Scenes and Ideas

by the a[...]

A Hundred Speeches from the Theatre

D0684699

By the same author

A Hundred Speeches from the Theatre

Scenes and Ideas

a selection from modern plays

Edited by

Rona Laurie BA (Hons), LGSM, LRAM

Evans Brothers Limited London

Published by Evans Brothers Limited
Montague House, Russell Square, London, W.C.1.

PR
1272
L37

Set in 10 on 12 point Georgian
and printed in Great Britain by
Northumberland Press Limited, Gateshead
57/6078   28020   PR3086

Contents

Acknowledgements

The Publishers are indebted to the following Authors, Publishers and Agents for permission to include extracts from six plays in this volume.

Willis Hall and Heinemann Educational Books Limited for *The Long and the Short and the Tall.*
John Osborne, Messrs. Faber & Faber and Margery Vosper Limited for *Luther.*
Keith Waterhouse and Willis Hall and Michael Joseph Limited for *Billy Liar.*
Arnold Wesker and Jonathan Cape Limited for *Roots.*
Wolf Mankowitz and Curtis Brown Limited for *The Bespoke Overcoat.*
Faber & Faber for *Christopher Columbus* by Louis MacNeice.

Introduction

One of the functions of the theatre is to shock people into thought and feeling; another is to amuse and delight them. The theatre is concerned with human life and its relation to society, and the scenes in this book have one thing in common: they all show people trying to grapple with the human problems that arise in the society in which they live.

It may be the problem, which many people have, of trying to communicate their ideas to their own family. Beatie Bryant, the central character in *Roots*, has this difficulty when she returns home from London full of the ideas and ideals which her friend Ronnie has given her and tries to introduce them to her own circle. She meets with little success, but of course all families are not so unresponsive as the Bryants.

The problem of a young man who resents authority is portrayed in *The Long and the Short and the Tall*, where we see Private Bamforth bored by the job in hand in a war that does not seem real to him. Billy Fisher in *Billy Liar* fights to get out of his complacent and unimaginative background by weaving a fantasy of lies and escaping into a Walter Mitty-like world of dreams; and although John Osborne's *Luther* is set in the sixteenth century, its central problem is just as pertinent today as it was then – the ways in which a man can fight for his own view of the truth and preserve his individuality.

In *The Bespoke Overcoat* we see Morry and Fender presenting a united although unsuccessful front to problems of poverty and old age. Finally, in Louis MacNeice's play for radio we see Christopher Columbus triumphant at last after his long struggle to convince indifferent and sceptical people of the truth of his vision of a new world in the west.

You will probably be reading these plays in a group and you may go on to act them. For that reason some notes on characterization have been given. If any of the scenes are to be performed in front of an audience, a few words of introduction from the producer or one of the cast would be helpful. It may be rewarding to perform one or two of them linked by the theme of man's relationship with the society around him.

Whatever method of approach is chosen, it is hoped that the dialogue will be brought to life and will provide food for discussion, and that those of you who do not know contemporary playwrights except through television performances will want to explore their work further and to tackle it for yourselves. The experience would be a stimulating one.

RONA LAURIE

Performing Rights

The Long and the Short and the Tall

Willis Hall

Before the fall of Singapore in the Second World War, a group of soldiers – not regulars – are on a patrol in the Malayan jungle. They stumble across a deserted store-hut and occupy it. They do not realise that the Japanese have started their offensive down the Malayan mainland and are, in fact, at this moment gradually infiltrating the area around them. And so the atmosphere at the beginning of the play is almost like that of a barrack room at home. The men are bored with their jobs and don't look on this patrol as an exercise of war which may cost them their lives, but rather as a tiresome chore. The realisation of danger is only gradually borne in upon them. A lone Japanese soldier finds them and they take him prisoner, but later when they are planning to escape he becomes an embarrassment to them. Finally one of them shoots him in a moment of panic, their position is discovered by the Japs and they are killed.

Despite the very special circumstances and setting of *The Long and the Short and the Tall*, neither of these is as important to the play as the characters of the soldiers themselves. Even in peacetime there are moments, in floods, earthquakes or during an epidemic, when one person or a group of people is brought face to face with danger. What is both important and interesting to observe is the reactions of those involved. In any group you may find people like Evans, Bamforth or Johnstone, and their reactions to a common danger would differ just as these soldiers' do.

From the play

Time: Late afternoon.
The curtain rises on the wooden-walled, palm-thatched, dingy in-
terior of a deserted store-hut in the Malayan jungle. The hut is set
back a few hundred yards from a tin mine which is now deserted.
There is a door in the rear wall with windows on either side looking
out on to the veranda and jungle beyond. The hut has been stripped
of everything of any value by the mine-workers before they fled.
All that remains is a rickety table and two chairs, centre stage, and
a form, stage right. We hear a short burst of heavy gunfire in the
distance – and then silence. A pause and then we hear the chirrup-
ing of crickets and the song of a bird in the jungle. A figure appears
at the left-hand window, looks cautiously inside and ducks away. A
moment later the door is kicked open and JOHNSTONE *stands framed*
in the doorway, holding a Sten gun at his hip. When the door was
kicked open the crickets and the birds ceased their song. JOHNSTONE
glances around the room and, finding it to be unoccupied, makes a
hand signal from the veranda. JOHNSTONE *returns into room and is*
joined a few seconds later by MITCHEM, *who also carries a Sten gun.*

JOHNSTONE (*shifts his hat to the back of his head and places his Sten*
on the table) All clear. Stinks like something's dead.

MITCHEM (*placing his Sten beside* JOHNSTONE'S) It'll do. To be going
on with. (*He crosses to the door and motions to the rest*
of the patrol.) Come on, then! Let's have you! Move it!
Move!
(*One by one the members of the patrol double into the*
room. With the exception of WHITAKER, *who carries the*
radio transmitter/receiver on his back, the men are
armed with rifles. SMITH *carries* WHITAKER'S *rifle. They*
are tired and dishevelled.)

JOHNSTONE Move yourselves! Gillo! Lacas! Lacas!
(*As the last member of the patrol enters the room*
MITCHEM *slams the door. The men stack their rifles in a*
corner of the hut and sit gratefully on the floor.
WHITAKER *takes off the 'set' and sets it up on the table.*
BAMFORTH *shrugs off his pack, places it as a pillow on the*
form, and makes himself comfortable.)

JOHNSTONE How long we here for?

MITCHEM (*glances at his watch*) Half an hour or so, and then we'll push off back. Better mount a guard. Two men on stag. Fifteen minute shifts.

JOHNSTONE Right. (*He notices* BAMFORTH *who is now fully stretched out.*) Bamforth! Bamforth!

BAMFORTH (*raises himself with studied unconcern*) You want me, Corp?

JOHNSTONE Get on your feet lad!

BAMFORTH What's up?

JOHNSTONE I said 'move'!

(BAMFORTH *pulls himself slowly to his feet.*)
You think you're on your holidays? Get your pack on!

BAMFORTH You going to inspect us, Corp?

JOHNSTONE Don't give me any of your mouth. Get your pack on! Smartish! Next time you keep it on till you hear different.

BAMFORTH (*heaves his pack on to one shoulder*) All right! O.K. All right.

JOHNSTONE Right on!

(BAMFORTH *glances across at* MITCHEM.)

MITCHEM You heard what he said.

BAMFORTH (*struggles the pack on to both shoulders. He speaks under his breath*) Nit!

(*There is a pause.* JOHNSTONE *crosses to face* BAMFORTH.)

JOHNSTONE What was that?

BAMFORTH Me. I only coughed.

MITCHEM O.K., Bamforth. Just watch it, son.

JOHNSTONE Too true, lad. Watch it. Watch it careful! I've had my bellyfull of you this time out. You watch your step. Put one foot wrong. Just one. I'll have you in the nick so fast your feet won't touch the ground. Just you move out of line, that's all.

BAMFORTH You threatening me, Corp?

JOHNSTONE I'm warning you!

BAMFORTH I got witnesses!

JOHNSTONE You'll have six months. The lot. I'll see to that, Bamforth. I'll have your guts. One foot wrong, as sure as God, I'll have your guts.

BAMFORTH Try. Try it on for size.

MITCHEM (*crosses to intervene*) Right. Pack it in. That's both of you.

(BAMFORTH *turns away from* JOHNSTONE.)
I want two men for guard. First stag. Two volunteers.
Come on, come on!

SMITH (*pulls himself to his feet*) First or second – what's the
odds?

MACLEISH (*follows suit*) It's all the same to me.

MITCHEM Better stay inside. Don't show yourselves. Cover the
front. If anything's to come it's coming from out there.
(MACLEISH *and* SMITH *take up their rifles and move across
to cover the windows.*)
How's the set?

WHITAKER (*looks up from tuning in the radio*) It's dead. Still dis.
U/S.[1] Can't get a peep. I think the battery's giving up.
Conking out.

BAMFORTH Now he tells us! Signals! Flipping signallers – I've shot
'em. Talk about up the creek without a paddle.

MITCHEM You got any suggestions, Bamforth –

BAMFORTH Only offering opinions.

MITCHEM Well don't! Don't bother. If we want opinions from you
we'll ask for them. From now on keep them to yourself.
Now, pay attention. All of you. We're sticking here for
half an hour at the most. After that we're – heading back
for camp. (*A murmur of relief from the men.*) Anybody
any questions?

EVANS Can we have a drag, Sarge?

MITCHEM Yeh. Smoke if you want. You can get the humpy off
your backs. Get what rest you can. Your best bet is to
grab some kip. It's a long way back. Another thing, you'd
better save your grub. I make it we'll get back before
tomorrow night – but just in case we don't, go steady on
the compo packs. O.K.?
(*There is a murmur of agreement from the men.*)
I want to have a sortie round. Outside. See how we're
fixed. Check up. Fancy a trot, Johnno?

JOHNSTONE Suits me.
(*The patrol remove their packs and place them on the
floor.* MITCHEM *and* JOHNSTONE *pick up and check their
Stens.*)

MITCHEM Keep at it on the set, Sammy son. Have another shot at
getting through.

[1] Useless.

WHITAKER (*puts on headphones*) Right, Sarge. Don't think it's going to do much good.

MITCHEM Keep bashing. Mac!

MACLEISH (*turns from window*) Aye?

MITCHEM We're having a stroll as far as the road. You're I/C.[1] We won't be long. As far as we know there's nothing in the area for miles – but if anything crops up – I mean, if you should see anything – don't shoot. Unless you've got to. Right?

MACLEISH Fair enough.

MITCHEM Ready, Johnno?

(JOHNSTONE *nods and follows* MITCHEM *to the door.*)

And keep your voices down, the lot of you.

JOHNSTONE Bamforth! That includes you!

BAMFORTH (*who has been delving into his pack*) I heard!

MITCHEM Come on.

(MITCHEM *opens door and goes out followed by* JOHNSTONE. *We see them move past window and disappear down the veranda steps.*)

BAMFORTH (*throwing down his pack in disgust*) The creep. The stupid nit!

(MITCHEM *and* JOHNSTONE *have returned.* MITCHEM *has told the men that in fifteen minutes they will start back towards camp. They believe the Japanese troops are miles off.*)

(BAMFORTH *and* EVANS *are now on guard.*)

MITCHEM Whitaker!

WHITAKER Sergeant?

MITCHEM Any joy on the set?

WHITAKER I got something through about five minutes ago, Sarge. I don't know what it was, though. Too faint to pick it up.

JOHNSTONE (*crossing to join* MITCHEM *and* WHITAKER) You got through to base, did you say, Whitaker?

WHITAKER No, Corp. I got something through though. I was telling the Sergeant. I picked up something, but I don't know what it was.

JOHNSTONE How much a week do they pay you for this, lad?

---

[1] I/C: in charge (military).

B

MITCHEM It's not his fault. The battery's dis. O.K., Sammy. Have another go. Better give it one more try.

WHITAKER (*sitting down at set*) Right. Sergeant. (*He tunes in the set behind following dialogue.*)

JOHNSTONE What do you reckon, Mitch?

MITCHEM What's that?

JOHNSTONE What he got?

MITCHEM Dunno. Suppose it must have been the camp. No one else in this area pushing out signals. With a wonky set he couldn't pick up any of the front line mobs from here. They're out of range. So it figures that it must have been the camp.

JOHNSTONE I'd like to put the boot in on the burk who dished us out with a U/S batt. S.O.B., that's all they are, the H.Q. men.

MITCHEM We'll sort that out when we get back.

JOHNSTONE I'd like to ram his pig-muck battery down his throat, that's all. Who was on duty in the battery shop?

MITCHEM It's no good flapping over that. We'll let him have another go and if nothing comes up we'll pack it in. Push off back. We've got a negative report. It doesn't make a lot of difference.

JOHNSTONE It could have been something else. It could have been important.

MITCHEM It isn't. So we can sort it out when we get back.
(JOHNSTONE *and* MITCHEM *turn and listen as* WHITAKER *attempts to make contact.*)

WHITAKER Blue Patrol to Red Leader. Blue Patrol calling Red Leader. Are you receiving me? Are you receiving me? Come in, Red Leader; come in, Red Leader. Over.
(WHITAKER *flicks to 'receive' and tunes in. Sound of interference held behind.* JOHNSTONE *and* MITCHEM *listen for a moment and then turn away.*)

JOHNSTONE Damn duff equipment! The whole damn issue's duff.

MITCHEM (*takes out a packet of cigarettes and offers one to* JOHNSTONE.) Fag?

JOHNSTONE (*taking the cigarette*) Ta. (*He takes a box of matches from his box, strikes one, offers a light to* MITCHEM, *then lights his own.*)

MITCHEM (*inhales deeply, then exhales*) Thanks.

JOHNSTONE Time do you reckon we'll get back?

MITCHEM Tomorrow? 'Bout eighteen hundred hours if we keep it up. Roll on. Roll on, let's get some kip.

JOHNSTONE If you get the chance. Kit inspection Saturday morning. What's the betting we end up on the square after that – C.O.'s. Parade?

MITCHEM Not this boy. I'm going to grab a weekend off and chuff the expense.

WHITAKER (*pushes the headphones on to the back of his head and turns in his chair*) Sarge!

MITCHEM (*turns*) Yeh?

WHITAKER Coming through again!

(MITCHEM *and* JOHNSTONE *cross to table and listen intently to the set.* WHITAKER *replaces headphones and tunes in.* MACLEISH *and* SMITH, *who have been talking together on the form, sit up and listen. There is an air of expectancy amongst the patrol. As* WHITAKER *fiddles with the controls the interference increases and dies away. A faint murmur of speech can be heard from the set.*)

WHITAKER There it is!

MITCHEM Come on, lad! Let's be having it.

EVANS Ask the C.O. if he loves me just as much as always, Whitto boy!

BAMFORTH Nobody loves you, you horrible Taff!

JOHNSTONE Shut up! Pack the talking in!

WHITAKER I've got it now!

(*The radio bursts into life. The voice of a Japanese radio operator comes through the set clearly.* WHITAKER *turns and looks in bewilderment at* MITCHEM. *These two are the first to realize the implications. There is a slight pause, stemming from surprise, then the patrol reacts with forced humour.*)

BAMFORTH You've got it, Whitto son, all right. You've got the ruddy Japs.

EVANS If that's the camp they're having rice for tea and my name's Tojo.

BAMFORTH Bring on the geisha girls!

MACLEISH A right ruddy radio operator you've turned out to be. Whitaker. You don't know whose side you're on.

MITCHEM (*leans across and switches off the set*) Pack the talking in, the lot of you! Right, Whitaker.

(WHITAKER, *who is staring in horror at the set, makes no reply.*)

Whitaker, I'm talking to you, lad!

(WHITAKER *looks up for the first time.*)

How strong's the battery? (*Pause.*) Come on, come on!

WHITAKER It's almost gone. The battery's nearly dead.

MITCHEM So what's your range at present? (*Pause.*) Whitaker, your range!

WHITAKER (*pulling himself together slightly*) It must be under fifteen miles. I can't get through to camp. It could be ten. It might be less.

(*With the exception of* EVANS *the patrol begins to comprehend.*)

EVANS Go on, Whitto boy! You're up the creek all over. The Japs are past Jalim Besar. It's twenty miles away at least.

SMITH We're all up the creek.

BAMFORTH Stroll on.

JOHNSTONE Evans! Bamforth! You're supposed to be on guard! Get on your posts!

(EVANS *and* BAMFORTH, *who have turned away from the windows during the above dialogue, return to their positions.*)

WHITAKER It was as clear as a bell! They could be sitting right on top of us!

MACLEISH Under fifteen miles away! So what's happened to the lads up country?

MITCHEM Shut up.

MACLEISH What's happened to the forward boys?

MITCHEM Shut up.

MACLEISH I've got my brother posted up out there!

MITCHEM Shut up! Johnno, check the Stens.

JOHNSTONE (*crossing to table where he checks* MITCHEM's *Sten and his own*) Right.

MITCHEM (*crossing to* MACLEISH) Now just shut up. It makes no difference now to you, lad, if your mother's kipping with a Jap. O.K.?

(MACLEISH *is about to burst into reply, but changes his mind and sits on form.*)

Then just remember that. Now listen. All of you. Evans, Bamforth, don't turn round. I want your eyes out there. You got that, both of you?

(BAMFORTH *and* EVANS *nod.*)

Then ram a round apiece up your spouts.

(BAMFORTH *and* EVANS *release the safety catches on their rifles, withdraw the bolts and slam them home.*)

O.K. Now put your safety catches on.

(BAMFORTH *and* EVANS *hesitate a moment and then comply*.)
O.K. That's fine. That's all we need. No more than that. (*He crosses centre stage to address the patrol*.) Fred Karno's mob. That's what you are. Fred Karno's mob. There's half of you been shooting off your mouths for days on end on how you'd fix the Japs. To listen to you talk you'd win the ruddy war on bread and jam. You've heard one slimy Nippo on the set and now you're having second thoughts. You make me laugh, that's what you do to me – make me want to laugh.
(JOHNSTONE *has now finished his examination of the Stens*.)
O.K., Johnno?
JOHNSTONE Both O.K.
MITCHEM (*to the patrol*) You've heard one Nippo on the set. That might mean anything at all. It might mean that they've broken through, up country, and are pouring down. If that's a fact then chuff your luck. That's all – just chuff your luck. They might be swarming out there now – like ants. And if they are and I'm with crumbs like you, I'm up the creek myself, and that's a fact.
(*The patrol murmurs uneasily*.)
But all you know so far is that you've heard a Nippo griping on the set. And that could mean that somewhere in this festering heat one lousy bunch of Japs have wriggled in behind our lines – that could be half a dozen men. It could be less than that. It could be half a dozen Joskins like yourselves. Six or seven – five or six – or even two or three poor helpless wet-nurse ginks who somewhere, close to here, are running round in circles, doing their nuts, because they've heard young Whitto pushing out a signal back to base. If that's the way things are with them, the bloke who's calling out the time for 'em has got my sympathy. I wish him luck. He's up to the short hairs in it like myself and so I wish him luck.
(*The confidence of the men has been largely restored – one or two are even amused*.)
I'll tell you what we're going to do. We're moving off. Right now.
(*Murmur of relief from the men*.)

We're going back. It's odds on that they're just a buck-shee bunch of Harries like yourselves. All the same, we're not waiting to find out. The orders for the movement back still stand. Evans, Bamforth, you'll stay on guard until the others have got their gear on and are ready to move off back.

(*The men begin to struggle into their webbing equipment.*)

JOHNSTONE Come on, then! Move yourselves! We've not got time to play about!

MITCHEM Macleish and Smith!

(MACLEISH *and* SMITH *pause in assembling their kit.*)

Soon as you've got into your gear relieve the two on guard and let them get theirs on.

(MACLEISH *and* SMITH *nod and return to their task.*)

Quick as you can.

JOHNSTONE (*picks up the Stens and hands one to* MITCHEM) You want me to lead off back?

MITCHEM (*nods*) Crack the whip a bit. Set a steady pace. I want to try and do it in one stint.

JOHNSTONE I'm with you.

BAMFORTH (*unnoticed by the others, he suddenly tenses himself and raises his rifle. He flicks off the safety catch and takes aim*) Sarge! Sarge!

MITCHEM (*sensing* BAMFORTH's *urgency*) Hold it, all of you!

(*The men are still and silent.*)

What's up?

BAMFORTH I thought I saw a movement down the track. It's there again!

MITCHEM (*to the patrol*) Get down! Get out of sight!

(*Apart from the two men on guard and* MITCHEM *the members of the patrol stoop below the level of the windows.*)

How many of them? Can you see?

BAMFORTH (*lowers his rifle*) No. Out of sight again. Behind the trees. Heading this way.

(MITCHEM, *his head down below window level, moves across the hut to join* BAMFORTH *at the window.* JOHNSTONE *moves across to join* EVANS.)

MITCHEM Which way they coming from?

BAMFORTH (*pointing*) Along the track. Down there. 'Bout fifty yards.

MITCHEM Evans?

EVANS Can't see a ruddy thing from here, Sarge. Not as far as that.

JOHNSTONE There's a clump of blasted bushes in the way.

MITCHEM Were they Japs?

BAMFORTH Might have been anything. Only had a glimpse.

MITCHEM Are you sure, Bamforth?

BAMFORTH Meaning what?

MITCHEM You saw anything at all, lad?

BAMFORTH You think I'm going round the bend!

MITCHEM All right. We'll take your word for it. If there is anyone down there they should come into sight again just by that bit of –

BAMFORTH (*nudges* MITCHEM *and points again*) A Jap!

MITCHEM I've got him. On his own. (*Turns slightly from window.*) Now keep still, all of you. This one's on his tod. Could be a scout. He hasn't spotted this place up to press. Got him, Johnno?

JOHNSTONE Can't see anything for this ruddy bush. Whereabouts?

MITCHEM Just less than fifty yards. Straight ahead. Got him, have you?

JOHNSTONE Not yet. What do you think he's on?

BAMFORTH He's – he's looking round for something. In the grass. Looking for something. Bending down.

JOHNSTONE Think he's found the trail, Mitch? Up to here?

MITCHEM Looks like that. Found something by the way he's carrying on.
(BAMFORTH *bursts into laughter.*)
Shut up!

BAMFORTH Found the trail! He's found the trail all right! He's found a place to have a crafty smoke.

EVANS He's what, Bammo?

BAMFORTH Having a drag. He's lighting up a fag. Well, the crafty old Nip. The skiving get. Caught red-handed. Nip down and ask him for a puff, Taff.

MITCHEM Of all the rotten luck. He would choose this place. We'll wait and see'f he pushes off.
(BAMFORTH *slowly raises his rifle and takes a careful aim.* MITCHEM *swings round and knocks the rifle out of aiming position.*)
I said no noise!

BAMFORTH I had him right between the cheeks! I couldn't miss! He's on his tod!

MITCHEM What gives you that idea? Do you think they march off by the dozen for a sly swallow?

JOHNSTONE What's happening?

BAMFORTH He's up. He's standing up and nicking out the nub. He's going back. The way he came. Stopped. Turning round. He's coming back. He's found the track up here. He's coming up.

MITCHEM Move it then, the rest of you. Let's have you over by the wall! And bring your gear.

(MACLEISH, WHITAKER *and* SMITH *pick up their rifles and the kit and scurry across to the rear wall of the hut.*)

(*Peering round window.*) Bamforth, Evans, down on deck!

(BAMFORTH *and* EVANS *drop below window level.*)

And stay there, all of you. There's just a chance he might not come inside. In case he does – Johnno –

(MITCHEM *indicates the door.* JOHNSTONE *nods and sidles across to stand by the door.* MITCHEM *peers round window.*)

If he should come in – you grab. Without a sound. I'll cover the outside in case. Still coming up. Close to the wall as you can. He might not see us yet.

WHITAKER (*notices the radio which is still standing on the table*) Sarge! The set!

MITCHEM Oh God, lad! Get it! Quick!

(WHITAKER *moves as if to cross to the table but changes his mind and hugs the wall in terror.*)

Get the set!

(WHITAKER *is still afraid to move.* SMITH *is about to fetch the radio when we hear the sound of feet on the wooden veranda.*)

Too late!

(*The members of the patrol squeeze up against the wall as* MITCHEM *edges away from the window out of sight.* JOHNSTONE *tenses himself. The Japanese soldier can be heard clattering on the veranda for several seconds before he appears at the left-hand window. He peers into the room, but fails to see the patrol and is just about to turn away when he notices the radio on the table. He stares at it for a short while and then moves out of sight as he crosses along the veranda towards the door. A further short pause.* JOHNSTONE *raises his hands in readi-*

*ness. The door opens and the Japanese soldier enters.
As he steps into the room* JOHNSTONE *lunges forward and
grabs the Japanese, putting an arm round his throat and
his free hand over the soldier's mouth.* MITCHEM, *holding the Sten at his hip, darts out of the door and covers
the jungle from the veranda.* JOHNSTONE *and the* PRISONER
struggle in the room.)

(MITCHEM *has decided that in spite of the apparent near-
ness of the Japanese troops, they will still attempt the
journey back to camp. They will take the* PRISONER *with
them, since he may be able to give valuable information.*
MACLEISH *and* SMITH *have gone down to the main track
to see whether there is any sign of the rest of the*
PRISONER'S *patrol.
The* PRISONER *is frightened but docile, and* BAMFORTH
makes friends with him.)

MITCHEM (*crossing to* EVANS) Where have them two got to?
EVANS No sign yet, Sarge.
  (MITCHEM *peers out of window.* BAMFORTH *takes out a
packet of cigarettes and puts one in his mouth. He
replaces the packet in his pocket and feels for a box of
matches as his glance falls on the* PRISONER, *who is looking up at him.* BAMFORTH *hesitates then transfers the
cigarette from his own mouth to the* PRISONER'S. *He takes
another cigarette for himself.* JOHNSTONE *rises and crosses
to* BAMFORTH. BAMFORTH *is still looking for a match as*
JOHNSTONE *takes out a box, strikes one and offers* BAM-
FORTH *a light.)*
BAMFORTH Ta.
  (JOHNSTONE *holds out the match for the* PRISONER. *As
the* PRISONER *leans across to get a light* JOHNSTONE *knocks
the cigarette from his mouth with the back of his hand.)*
  What's that in aid of?
JOHNSTONE He gets permission first!
BAMFORTH I gave him it!
JOHNSTONE Since when have you been calling out the time!
BAMFORTH I don't ask you before I give a bloke a fag!
JOHNSTONE This one you do!
BAMFORTH Who says!

JOHNSTONE I do, lad! (*Making a sudden grab for the* PRISONER *and attempting to tear open his breast pocket.*) I'll fix his photos for the Herb as well!

MITCHEM (*turns*) Corporal Johnstone!

BAMFORTH (*drops the bayonet and clutches* JOHNSTONE *by his jacket lapels. He brings his knee up in* JOHNSTONE's *groin and, as* JOHNSTONE *doubles forward,* BAMFORTH *cracks his forehead against the bridge of* JOHNSTONE's *nose*) Have that!

MITCHEM (*crossing towards the fight*) Bamforth!

(BAMFORTH, *unheeding, strikes* JOHNSTONE *in the stomach and pushes him to the floor.*)

JOHNSTONE (*pulling himself to his feet*) All right. You've done it this time, Bamforth! You've shot your load. As sure as God you'll get three years for that.

BAMFORTH (*picks up bayonet*) You try and make it stick.

MITCHEM You're on a charge, Bamforth. You're under open arrest.

BAMFORTH He started it!

MITCHEM Tell that to the C.O.

EVANS (*raising his rifle*) Sarge! There's someone coming up the track!

MITCHEM (*crosses to window*) Whereabouts?

EVANS Just coming through the trees.

(JOHNSTONE *picks up his Sten and crosses to join* WHITAKER.)

MITCHEM It's all right. It's Macleish and Smith. Cover them up the track.

JOHNSTONE (*aiming the Sten*) I've got them.

EVANS Looks as if they're in a hurry over something.

(*A pause before we hear* MACLEISH *and* SMITH *clatter up on to the veranda.* MITCHEM *opens the door and they enter the room. They lean against the wall, exhausted.*)

MITCHEM Anybody after you?

(MACLEISH *shakes his head.*)

What's up then?

EVANS What's the hurry, Smudger boy? You look as if you've had the whole of the Japanese army on your tail.

SMITH (*out of breath*) We have. Near enough.

MITCHEM Sit down a tick.

(SMITH *and* MACLEISH *cross to the table and sit down.* MITCHEM *crosses to join them.*)

Now, come on – give. Let's be having it.

MACLEISH (*regaining his breath*) They've broken through. In strength. There's hundreds of them moving down the main trail back.

MITCHEM Go on.

SMITH They must have come through our defence lines like a dose of salts. They're pouring down. Happy as a lot of sand boys. Not a mark on any one of them. Up front the whole damn shoot's collapsed.

MITCHEM You weren't spotted?

MACLEISH (shakes his head) They're not even looking for anybody. They seem to know they've got this area to themselves. Smudge and myself got down in the long grass. They've got no scouts out. Nothing. Just strolling down the trail as if they owned the jungle.

MITCHEM Do you think they'll find this place?

MACLEISH Not yet awhile. We watched about a company march past. There was a break then in the file. We managed to cover up the entrance of the trail up here.

SMITH We stuffed it up with bits of branch and stuff.

MITCHEM Good.

MACLEISH The next batch came along as we were finishing. We patched up what we could and scooted back.

JOHNSTONE So what happens now?

MITCHEM It's put the kybosh on the journey back. We can't move out of here just yet, and that's a certainty.

MACLEISH You never saw so many Japs. There must be at least a thousand of them now between ourselves and base. We're right behind their forward lines.

MITCHEM (crosses downstage and turns) Let's say, for now, they march without a stop. That brings them close up on the camp before tomorrow night. If they've got stuff up in the air to back them up – and if they don't know back at base they've broken through – the base mob gets wiped up.

MACLEISH But they'll know by now the Japs are through.

MITCHEM We can't count on that.

JOHNSTONE If the main road's free, they'll have heavy transport loads of Nips chugging down before tomorrow.

MITCHEM Let's hope the Engineers have sewn that up. They'll have it mined at least. No, this is the back way in. Cross country – and it's hard graft cutting trail – they'll have to do the lot on foot.

JOHNSTONE So?

MITCHEM So that means we can put the blocks on them. We get there first.

JOHNSTONE You think the Japs are going to open ranks and let us pass?

MITCHEM What's the time now? (*He glances at his watch.*) It'll be dark in just over an hour. We might make it then.

JOHNSTONE And so you think we stand a chance at creeping through a regiment of ruddy Nips!

MITCHEM What's your suggestion?

JOHNSTONE We haven't got a chance.

MITCHEM We've got no choice. We might make it in the dark and in that shrub. They'll be blundering about themselves. At least we know the way – we've done it coming up. It's all new ground to them. We might creep through.

JOHNSTONE (*indicating the* PRISONER) What? With him in tow?

MITCHEM (*glancing across at the* PRISONER) No. We're ditching him. Whitaker!

WHITAKER (*turning at window*) Sarge?

MITCHEM (*indicating set*) Come on. You'd better give it one more try.

WHITAKER I don't think it'll do any good, Sarge. The battery's nigh on stone dead.

MITCHEM Try it, lad! Don't argue. Relieve him, Smith.
(SMITH *crosses to take* WHITAKER's *place at the window as* WHITAKER *crosses to table and sits at set. He switches on to 'transmit' and pauses.*)
Come on, lad! Get on with it! We haven't time to mess about.

WHITAKER (*turning in his chair to speak to* MITCHEM) If there are any Japs near here switched to receive they'll get a fix on us.

MITCHEM That can't be helped. Come on, come on!

WHITAKER (*putting on headphones and tuning in*) Blue Patrol to Red Leader. Blue Patrol to Red Leader. Are you receiving me? Are you receiving me? Come in Red Leader. Come in, Red Leader. Over. (WHITAKER *switches to 'receive' and tunes in. We hear the crackle of interference.*) Nothing yet.

MITCHEM Come on, Sammy son, come on.

WHITAKER (*adjusting tuning dial*) There's something here.
(*The interference dies away and we here the voice of the Japanese radio operator as before.*)

It's the Jap transmitting. Same as before.

MITCHEM Get off the ruddy line, you Nip!

(*The voice continues in Japanese for a few seconds and then stops. It continues in taunting broken English.*)

OPERATOR Johnee! Johnee! British Johnee! We – you – come – to get. We – you – come – to – get.

(WHITAKER *starts up in fear and* MITCHEM *pushes him back into his chair. The patrol turn and look at the* PRISONER. *The* PRISONER, *noting that all attention is centred on himself, and feeling that he is expected to entertain the patrol, raises his hands in the air and slowly places them on his head. He smiles round blandly in search of approbation.*)

CURTAIN

Understanding the play

Characters

When trying to bring these scenes to life, informal discussion is important at every stage. After you have read the excerpts given here, you should discuss the action, the characters and the various problems involved in making the dialogue 'come alive'. You might ask yourselves questions like these:

1 How can the soldiers suggest the heat and discomfort of their situation:

(a) in their actions, the way they move;

(b) in their voices, the rate at which they speak and pick up cues[1]?

2 From the evidence in the three scenes, do you think that Corporal Johnstone is a good disciplinarian?

3 What do the men think of him?

4 What might be the problems of a sergeant in this situation?

5 How does Sergeant Mitchem cope with these problems?

6 Do you think that he enjoys his responsibility?

7 Bamforth has been described as a 'barrack-room lawyer'. What does this term mean? Do you agree with this description of him?

8 Why do you think Bamforth is so bitter and resentful of authority?

9 What is Johnstone's attitude to Bamforth?

10 Macleish is a Scot, Evans a Welshman. How can the actors playing these parts avoid turning them into a 'stage Scotsman' and a 'stage Welshman'?

11 Whitaker is described as being fussy and priggish. How can the actor suggest these qualities without making him a figure of fun?

12 The Japanese soldier has no lines to speak. How can the actor playing this part suggest:

(a) the thoughts and feelings;

(b) the nationality of the character?

---

[1] The word 'cue' has been in use for many years. Shakespeare used it in *A Midsummer Night's Dream*, when Bottom. awaking from sleep. says: "When my cue comes, call me, and I will answer." The last few words spoken by the actor in a speech form the cue for the next actor to speak. The cue acts as a warning to the next actor that it is now his turn to take up the dialogue.

How the play is built up

Introduction of the characters: By now you have probably formed your own ideas about what the characters are like. In the first excerpt, the main characters are introduced. You might read it again, this time noticing how the playwright manages to suggest right from the beginning the differences between these men. Ask yourselves:

1 *How do Bamforth's first actions show what kind of a person he is?*
2 *What do we learn from Johnstone's first lines about his attitude to the rest of the patrol?*
3 *How does Mitchem show that he is the one in command?*

Explanation of the situation: As well as introducing the characters, the playwright has to make us realize, right from the beginning, what sort of situation these men are in. Try to find lines in the first scene in which we are told:

(a) that the men are tired and fed up;
(b) that they are growing increasingly uneasy about their plight.

Development of the plot: Many playwrights today are not concerned with telling a story. They do not consider it important that a play should have a beginning, a middle and an end. Viewers of television plays often say that they feel angry and frustrated when a play has no definite ending, with the story-ends tied up neatly. They say that they feel left in the air. But such plays, when they are well-written, leave room for the imagination to work, and it is not a bad thing for us to have to think very hard about the ideas in the play and perhaps to try to work out for ourselves what happens to the characters afterwards. If the dialogue has been good, we can imagine what these characters are like as human beings, even though we have not seen them doing very much. In fact, very little may seem to have happened in the play. There has been practically no development of plot. (Some of Harold Pinter's plays are of this kind, and later in the book we shall be considering a play of this type by Wolf Mankowitz.)

However, some modern playwrights prefer to write plays with a more definite framework and a clear story-line. Willis Hall's *The Long and the Short and the Tall* has a definite beginning, middle and end and tells a story. That does not mean that there is no room for the imagination to work, even though there is not the same freedom to interpret the playwright's intentions as there is in the other kind of play. In this play, we have to try to imagine and to understand the feelings of these very different characters. Remember that these are green soldiers – not experienced ones (apart from Sergeant Mitchem and Corporal Johnstone) – and their reactions to what to them is an unfamiliar situation of danger would not be the same as those of regular, seasoned troops. There would not be so much hiding of the man's real character behind the façade of a uniform as there would be with regular soldiers.

First of all we have to try to imagine how we ourselves would react to the changing situations in the play. Then we have to try to understand the various characters from the evidence of what they do, what they say and how the other characters react to them and talk about them.

Look at the second excerpt and ask yourselves:

1 At what point in it is the situation changed from what it was at the beginning of the play?
2 How does the playwright build up suspense and excitement before the next incident in the story?
3 What is the next incident?

The use and meaning of dramatic climax

If a play consisted merely of a series of events strung together, it would become very dull, and readers and audience would grow bored. How does the playwright avoid this; how does he try to keep us continually 'forward in our seats'?

One way of holding the audience's interest is by showing the changes in the characters caused by the events in the plot and their reactions to these events. These changes create the development of the characters which in time causes the story to change and progress. Unless the characters developed, we shouldn't really believe in them, and they would remain merely puppets of the author.

Another way of holding interest is for the events to lead up to one very important moment, which can excite the audience and which may change the direction of the story completely. We call these dramatic moments 'climaxes'. They sometimes occur in the middle of a scene. Very often you find them at the end of an act, so that the audience waits eagerly to see what will happen in the next act. Sometimes, there is one big climax at the end of a play; sometimes, a series of smaller ones throughout.

1 In the second excerpt, can you find one small climax and one bigger one?

2 There is a big climax in the third excerpt. What is it?

3 Which do you think is the most important climax of all?

Bringing the play to life

It is useful and interesting to know how a play is built up by the playwright. A knowledge of how he works will help us when we come to read or act his play. For example, knowing where the climaxes come will help us to shape and control a reading. But it is not enough to know where the climaxes occur; we must be able to convey them in our acting. How can we do this?

There are a number of different ways and it is important to find the right one for each different climax as it comes along. You could speak faster as you build up to the climax, leaving shorter pauses between speeches. We call this picking up cues quickly. You could speak more and more loudly and with more and more feeling as you approach the climax of a scene. Climaxes have been built up, too, by the characters speaking more and more quietly but with great concentration. Experiment to find out which methods work best for your own scenes. The proof of the pudding is in the eating, and you will soon hear for yourselves when a climax has come off and when it hasn't.

There are many methods of bringing a play to life in the classroom; two only are described here. You will probably have other ideas of your own.

A 'live' dramatic performance

Here the emphasis will be on action and situation. Even in a classroom where there is not much space, a great deal can be done to create atmosphere. By atmosphere, I mean the suggestion of the mood, time and location of the play. This is done in a performance by means of the stage setting, lighting, costume and make-up, music and sound effects. In the classroom, atmosphere can be created by the use of tape-recorded music and sound effects, and you will find that this stimulates the acting.

The Long and the Short and the Tall, in particular, lends itself to being acted in cramped surroundings: the jungle hut can be a very small one. The fact that there is no scenery makes the actors' and the director's task more challenging. (Remember, too, that Shakespeare's own company and the other Elizabethan dramatists all worked with the minimum of props[1] and scenery.) It might be interesting to divide the class into two groups, each with its own director (or you could have different directors for each scene) and let each group work out its own interpretation. Then each could watch the other's effort and the resulting discussion should be most informative and, it is to be hoped, constructive.

If you decided to give these scenes a public performance – acting them for another class or parents to watch – it would be helpful to the audience if you had a narrator, who could be another soldier, to introduce the play, to link the episodes and to round the whole thing off. You could try your hand in class at composing these pieces of narration, and use the most effective ones.

A tape-recorded performance

Here the emphasis will be more on character and less on action than in the 'live' performance. Great care needs to be taken with the casting. Whereas, in the first method, personality, acting ability and appearance should be considered, here it is the *voice* which should guide you first of all when allocating parts; though acting ability is important here, too, of course.

You will notice, in this play, that different accents and dialects are called for; the men come from all parts of the country. You may have people in your class who actually come from the same district as one or other of these characters. If not, it would be interesting to try to reproduce the various accents required – Scots, Welsh, North Country and so on. You have opportunities of studying all kinds of accents in television documentaries and interviews. But remember, when adopting an alien accent for a play, that a little goes a long way; and try not to overdo it and become a 'stage Welshman' or a 'stage Scotsman'.

This play lends itself to recorded performance particularly well. The different accents of the various characters make them easily identifiable and the device, so often employed in radio plays, of making the characters constantly refer to one another by name is not needed.

---

[1] PROPS: short for 'properties', is the term used in the theatre to describe anything that is either brought on to the stage by the actors (for example, a suitcase, a parcel, a walking-stick) or handled by them when they are on (for example, a document, a revolver, a cigarette case).

Sound effects can help to create atmosphere. Which ones could you devise to suggest the heat, the jungle vegetation and the animals or birds you might hear? (Remember that sound effects should only be a *background* to the actors' voices.) You might have someone in your class who is clever at creating effects and mixing them. It is probably best, after rehearsing the dialogue, to record it in sections as you feel each has reached a reasonable standard; and then join all the sections together.

Criticism

Whichever method you choose, it is useful after a performance of any kind, in the classroom or anywhere else, to discuss and criticise what you have done. Here are some of the questions that you could ask yourselves:

1 Did we come anywhere near what we hoped to achieve?
2 If it did not succeed as a whole, did any bits of it really seem to come to life?
3 Did we sound like real people or simply like actors pretending to be real people?
4 Did the climaxes we aimed for come off?
5 If we were to go through the whole exercise again, would we do any of it differently?
6 Where did our directors help the actors particularly?
7 Were the sound effects convincing?

Follow-up

Having studied these excerpts from Act One, I hope you will want to go on to read the whole play and to find out something about Willis Hall. He has written many radio, television and film scripts as well as other plays. Another of his plays, *Billy Liar*, which he wrote in collaboration with Keith Waterhouse, is represented later in this book.

After working on *The Long and the Short and the Tall*, why not try improvising your own play involving a similar group of characters in different circumstances. Here are some possibilities:

1 *Resistance workers in enemy-occupied territory have been captured and pushed into a cellar. They plan to escape. All react differently to the escape plan proposed.*
2 *A group of young people have witnessed a wage-snatch. The criminals kidnap them, shut them up in a guarded room in an empty house and try to buy their silence.*
3 *A group of pot-holers have been trapped by rising floodwater and are waiting for a new shaft to be drilled.*
4 *A group of miners have been trapped by a fall of coal. Their only communication with the surface is through a speaking-tube. There is danger of further falls.*

In each of these scenes, make sure that you have an assorted group of characters whose reactions would all be different. Try to contrive at least two incidents with a period of suspense and excitement in between.

Luther

John Osborne

The Long and the Short and the Tall told the story of men faced with a common danger. We were interested in the different reactions within a group. John Osborne's play *Luther* describes the fight of one man against an organization.

The scene is Germany, early in the sixteenth century. Martin Luther, a monk and scholar who has been described as the father of revolutions, is struggling against the corruption and slackness of the church of his day. He is bitterly opposed to many of the established customs of the church, and in particular to the practice of selling indulgences. These were letters in sealed envelopes, supposed to come from the Pope, offering forgiveness of sins to anyone who bought them, and many of the clergy had become successful in selling large numbers of them to the public. One such is John Tetzel, a Dominican friar with a powerful personality and persuasive tongue, whom Osborne shows hawking indulgences to a crowd gathered in the market place. He says: 'Not only am I empowered to give you these letters of pardon for the sins you've already committed. I can give you pardon for the sins you haven't even committed – but which, however, you intend to commit!' And, later: 'As soon as your money rattles in the box and the cash bell rings, the soul flies out of purgatory and sings!' This scene ends with 'the sound of coins chattering like rain into a great coffer.'

Martin Luther, then, was openly defying the church when he said that indulgences had no power to remove guilt. But he was not fighting the church on this issue alone. He proclaimed that man is saved by faith, and not by good deeds. He tells the people: 'You must be made to know that there's no security at all, either in indulgences, or holy busywork or anywhere in the world.'

In 1517, Luther nailed his Ninety-Six Theses against indulgences to the door of Wittenberg Castle Church. In the next year, having been accused of heresy, he wrote to the Pope to defend his ideas. A meeting was arranged with Cardinal Cajetan, the Papal Legate in Germany. It is this meeting that Osborne re-creates in the scene that follows.

From the play

The scene is a Palace in Augsburg, in October 1518. CARDINAL CAJETAN, *a man of about fifty, but youthful in outlook, has been talking with* TETZEL, *who is outraged at* MARTIN'S *open defiance of the Church.* TETZEL *goes out and returns with* MARTIN, *who advances, prostrates himself, his face to the ground before* CAJETAN. CAJETAN *makes a motion and* MARTIN *rises to a kneeling position, where* CAJETAN *studies him.*

CAJETAN (*courteous*) Please stand up, Dr Luther. So you're the one they call the excessive doctor. You don't look excessive to me. Do you feel very excessive?

MARTIN (*conscious of being patronized*) It's one of those words which can be used like a harness on a man.

CAJETAN How do you mean?

MARTIN I mean it has very little meaning beyond traducing him.

CAJETAN Quite. There's never been any doubt in my mind that you've been misinterpreted all round and, as you say, traduced. Well, what a surprise you are! Here was I expecting to see some doddering old theologian with dust in his ears who could be bullied into a heart attack by Tetzel here in half an hour. And here you are, as gay and sprightly as a young bull. How old are you, my son?

MARTIN Thirty-four, most worthy Father.

CAJETAN Tetzel, he's a boy – you didn't tell me! And how long have you been wearing your doctor's ring?

MARTIN Five years.

CAJETAN So you were only twenty-nine! Well, obviously, everything I've heard about you is true – you must be a very remarkable young man. I wouldn't have believed there was one doctor in the whole of Germany under fifty. Would you, Brother John?

TETZEL I certainly wouldn't.

CAJETAN What is surprising, frankly, is that they allowed such an honour to be conferred on anyone so young and inexperienced as a man must inevitably be at twenty-nine. (*He smiles to let his point get home.*) Your father must be a proud man.

MARTIN *(irritated)* Not at all, I should say he was disappointed and constantly apprehensive.

CAJETAN Really? Well, that's surely one of the legacies of parenthood to offset the incidental pleasures. Now then, to business. I was saying to Tetzel, I don't think this matter need take up very much of our time. But, before we do start, there's just one thing I would like to say, and that is I was sorry you should have decided to ask the Emperor for safe conduct. That was hardly necessary, my son, and it's a little – well, distressing to feel you have such an opinion of us, such a lack of trust in your mother church and in those who have, I can assure you, your dearest interests at heart.

MARTIN *(out-manoeuvred)* I –

CAJETAN *(kindly)* But never mind all that now, that's behind us and, in the long run, it's unimportant, after all, isn't it? Your vicar general has come with you, hasn't he?

MARTIN He's outside.

CAJETAN I've known Staupitz for years. You have a wonderful friend there.

MARTIN I know. I have a great love for him.

CAJETAN And he has for you, too, I know. Oh, my dear, dear son. This is such a ridiculous, unnecessary business for us all to be mixed up in. It's such a tedious, upsetting affair and what purpose is there in it? Your entire order in Germany has been brought into disgrace. I have my job to do and, make no mistake, it isn't all honey for an Italian legate in your country. You know how it is, people are inclined to resent you. Nationalist feeling and all that – which I respect – but it does complicate one's task to the point where this kind of issue thrown in for good measure simply makes the whole operation impossible. You know what I mean? I mean, there's your Duke Frederick, an absolutely fair, honest man if ever there was one, and one his holiness values and esteems particularly. Well, he instructed me to present him with the Golden Rose of Virtue, so you can see. As well as even more indulgences for his Castle church. But what happens now? Because of all this unpleasantness and the uproar it's caused throughout Germany, the duke's put in an extremely difficult position about accepting it. Naturally, he wants to do the right thing

by everyone. But he's not going to betray you or anything like that, however much he's set his heart on that
Golden Rose, all these years. So, you see, my dear son,
what a mess we are in. Now, what are we going to do?
Um? The duke is unhappy. I am unhappy, his holiness
is unhappy and, you, my son, you are unhappy.

MARTIN *(formal, as if it were a prepared speech)* Most worthy
Father, in obedience to the summons of his papal holiness and, in obedience to the orders of my gracious lord,
the Elector of Saxony, I have come before you as a
submissive and dutiful son of the holy Christian church
and if I have been wrong, to submit to your instruction
in the truth.

CAJETAN *(impatiently)* My son, you have upset all Germany with
your dispute about indulgences. I know you're a very
learned doctor of the Holy Scriptures and that you've
already aroused some supporters. But, if you wish to
remain a member of the church and to find a gracious
father in the pope, you'd better listen. I have here, in
front of me, three propositions which, by the command
of our holy father, Pope Leo the Tenth, I shall put to
you now. First, you must admit your faults and retract
all your errors and sermons. Secondly, you must promise
to abstain from propagating your opinions at any time
in the future. And, thirdly, you must behave generally
with greater moderation and avoid anything which
might cause offence or grieve and disturb the church.

MARTIN May I be allowed to see the pope's instruction?

CAJETAN No, my dear son, you may not. All you are required to
do is confess your errors, keep a strict watch on your
words and not go back like a dog to his vomit. Then,
once you have done that, I have been authorized by our
most holy father to put everything to rights again.

MARTIN I understand all that. But I'm asking you to tell me
where I have erred.

CAJETAN If you insist. *(Rattling off, very fast.)* Just to begin with,
here are two propositions you have advanced and which
you will have to retract before anything else. First, the
treasure of indulgences does not consist of the sufferings
and torments of our Lord Jesus Christ. Second, the man
who receives the holy sacrament must have faith in the
grace that is presented to him. Enough?

MARTIN   I rest my case entirely on Holy Scriptures.

CAJETAN   The pope alone has power and authority over all those things.

MARTIN   Except Scripture.

CAJETAN   Including Scripture. What do you mean?

TETZEL   Only the pope has the power to interpret the meaning of Scripture. The pope's judgment cannot err, whether it concerns the Christian faith or anything that has to do with the salvation of the human race.

MARTIN   That sounds like your thesis.

TETZEL   Burned in the market-place by your students in Wittenberg – thank you very much.

MARTIN   I assure you, I had nothing to do with that.

CAJETAN   Of course. Brother John wasn't suggesting you had.

TETZEL   Why, your heresy isn't even original. It's no different from Wyclif or Hus.

CAJETAN   True enough, but we mustn't try to deprive the learned doctor of his originality. But it is original so long as it originated in you, the virgin heretic.

TETZEL   The time'll come when you'll have to defend yourself before the world and then every man can judge for himself who's the heretic and schismatic. People like you always go too far, thank heaven. I give you a month, Brother Martin, to roast yourself.

MARTIN   You've had your thirty pieces of silver. For the sake of Christ, why don't you betray someone?

CAJETAN   (to TETZEL) Perhaps you should join Staupitz.

TETZEL   Very well, your eminence. (He bows and goes out.)

CAJETAN   In point of fact, he gets eighty guilden a month plus expenses.

MARTIN   What about his vow of poverty?

CAJETAN   Like most brilliant men, my son, you have an innocent spirit. I've also just discovered that he has managed to father two children. So there goes another vow. Bang! But it'll do him no good, I promise you. You've made a hole in that drum for him. I may say there's a lot of bad feelings among the Dominicans about you. I should know – because I'm their general. It's only natural they're accustomed to having everything their own way. The Franciscans are a grubby, sentimental lot, on the whole, and mercifully ignorant as well. But your people seem to be running alive with scholars and would-be-politicians.

MARTIN I'd no idea that my theses would ever get such publicity.

CAJETAN Really now!

MARTIN But it seems they've been printed over and over again and circulated well, to an extent I'd never dreamed of.

CAJETAN Oh yes, they've been circulated and talked about where-ever men kneel to Christ.

MARTIN Most holy Father, I honour the Holy Roman church and I shall go on doing so. I have sought after the truth and everything I have said I still believe to be right and true and Christian. But I am a man and I may be deceived, so I am willing to receive instruction where I have been mistaken.

CAJETAN (angrily) Save your arrogance, my son, there'll be a better place to use it. I can have you sent to Rome and let any of your German princes try to stop me! He'll find himself standing outside the gates of Heaven like a leper.

MARTIN (stung) I repeat, I am here to reply to all the charges you may bring against me.

CAJETAN No, you're not.

MARTIN I am ready to submit my theses to the universities of Basle, Freibourg-in-Breisgau, Louvain or Paris –

CAJETAN I'm afraid you've not grasped the position. I'm not here to enter into a disputation with you, now or at any other time. The Roman church is the apex of the world, spiritual and temporal, and it may constrain with its secular arm any who have once received the faith and gone astray. Surely I don't have to remind you that it is not bound to use reason to fight and destroy rebels. (He sighs.) My son, it's getting late. You must retract. Believe me, I simply want to see this business ended as quickly as possible.

MARTIN Some interests are furthered by finding truth, others by destroying it. I don't care – what pleases or displeases the pope. He is a man.

CAJETAN (wearily) Is that all?

MARTIN He seems a good man, as popes go. But it's not much for a world that sings not for reformation.

CAJETAN My dear friend, think carefully and see if you can't see some way out of all this. Retract, my son, the holy Father prays for it –

MARTIN But won't you discuss – ?

CAJETAN   Discuss! I've not discussed with you and I don't intend
to. If you want a disputation, I dare say Eck will take
care of you –

MARTIN   John Eck? The Chancellor of Ingoldstadt?

CAJETAN   I suppose you don't think much of him?

MARTIN   He knows theology.

CAJETAN   He has a universal reputation in debate.

MARTIN   It's understandable. He has a pedestrian style and a
judicial restraint and that'll always pass off as wisdom
to most men.

CAJETAN   You mean he's not original, like you.

MARTIN   I'm not an original man. Why, I'm not even a teacher
and I'm scarcely even a priest. I know Jesus Christ
doesn't need my labour or my services.

CAJETAN   All right, Martin, I will argue with you if you want me
to, or at least, I'll put something to you, because there is
something more than your safety or your life involved,
something bigger than you and I talking together in
this room at this time. Oh, it's fine for someone like you
to criticize and start tearing down Christendom, but tell
me this, what will you build in its place?

MARTIN   An infected place is best scoured out and so you pray
for healthy tissue and something sturdy and clean for
what was crumbling and full of filth.

CAJETAN   My dear son, can't you see? My son, you'll destroy the
perfect unity of the world.

MARTIN   Someone always prefers what's withered and infected.
But it should be cauterized as honestly as one knows
how.

CAJETAN   And how honest is that? There's something I'd like to
know. Suppose you did destroy the pope. What do you
think would become of you?

MARTIN   I don't know.

CAJETAN   Exactly, you wouldn't know what to do because you
need him, Martin, you need to hunt him more than he
needs his silly wild boar. Well? There have always been
popes and there always will be, even if they're called
something else. They'll have them for people like you.
You're not a good old revolutionary, my son, you're
just a common rebel, a very different animal. You don't
fight like the pope, not because he's too big, but because
for your needs he's not big enough.

MARTIN My general's been gossiping.

CAJETAN (*contemptuous*) I don't need Staupitz to explain you to me. Why, some deluded creature might even come to you as a leader of their revolution, but you don't want to break rules, you want to make them. I've read some of your sermons on faith. Did you know all they say to me?

MARTIN No.

CAJETAN They say, I am a man struggling for certainty, struggling insanely like a man in a fit, an animal trapped to the bone with doubt.

(MARTIN *seems about to have a physical struggle with himself.*)

Don't you see what could happen out of all this? Men could be cast out and left to themselves for ever, helpless and frightened.

MARTIN Your eminence, forgive me. I'm tired after my journey – I think I might faint soon.

CAJETAN That's what would become of them without their mother church – with all its imperfections, Peter's rock, without it they'd be helpless and unprotected. Allow them their sins, their petty indulgences, my son, they're unimportant to the comfort we receive.

MARTIN (*somewhat hysterical*) Comfort! It – doesn't concern me!

CAJETAN We live in thick darkness and it grows thicker. How will men find God if they are left to themselves, each man abandoned and only known to himself?

MARTIN They'll have to try.

CAJETAN I beg of you, my son, I beg of you. Retract.

(*Pause.*)

MARTIN Most holy Father, I cannot.

(*Pause.*)

CAJETAN You look ill. You had better go and rest. (*Pause.*) Naturally, you will be released from your order.

MARTIN I –

CAJETAN Yes?

MARTIN As you say, your eminence. Will you refer this matter to the pope for his decision?

CAJETAN Assuredly. Send in Tetzel.

(MARTIN *prostrates himself and then kneels.* CAJETAN *is distressed but in control.*)

You know, Martin, a time will come when a man will

no longer be able to say 'I speak Latin and am a Christian' and go his way in peace. There will come frontiers, frontiers of all kinds – between men – and there'll be no end to them.

(MARTIN *rises and goes out.* TETZEL *returns.*)

TETZEL Yes?

CAJETAN No, of course he didn't – that man hates himself. And if he goes to the stake, Tetzel, you can have the pleasure of inscribing it; he could only love others.

CURTAIN

Understanding the play

Characters

Here are brief descriptions of the three men:
MARTIN LUTHER: painfully honest, shrinking from comfort both for himself and for other people. He is courageous, blunt, stubborn, full of intelligence and learning.

1 Can you find speeches from the scene that illustrate any of these sides of Luther's character?
2 What is your opinion of the man from the evidence in the scene?

CAJETAN: Rome's highest representative in Germany. He has a shrewd, broad outlook. He is intelligent, even charming.

1 Where does he show his shrewdness in this scene?
2 He shows his breadth of outlook in one of his speeches to Martin towards the end of the interview. Can you find the speech?

JOHN TETZEL: vulgar, obstinate and prejudiced.

Which lines, do you think, show his vulgarity either in thought, or choice of words, or both?

How the play is built up

In the first excerpt in this book, we saw how the playwright sets the scene and introduces the characters at the beginning of a play. The scene between Luther, Cajetan and Tetzel occurs in the second part of John Osborne's play, however, so that a fresh set of questions arises and we can see how the playwright handles a situation in which there is little physical action but a tremendous clash of personalities and of ideas. Martin, of course, represents the new spirit of Reformation, whereas Cajetan speaks for 'the Establishment' – for the traditions of the Church and for the authority of the Pope.

1 In the stage directions, we read that Martin is conscious of being patronized after Cajetan's first lines. Why do you think that he feels this?

2 Later, Cajetan uses Martin's youth as a weapon against him. Do you think that this is fair?

3 When does Martin begin to stand up to him?

4 What is Cajetan's reaction to this?

5 Luther and Cajetan clash on the question of the interpretation of Holy Scriptures. What are Luther's views on the Pope's powers?

6 What are Cajetan's views?

7 Why do you think Cajetan suggests that Tetzel should leave them?

8 You have discussed 'climax' in playwriting in connection with the first play in this book. Can you find the main climax in this scene?

Bringing the play to life

Although there are only three characters in this scene, your whole group could work on different aspects of it. You might divide your-selves like this:

Four groups of three actors and one director.

Eight people doing research on the period and writing an intro-duction.

Four people finding and recording music for the beginning and end of the scene.

Four people designing a possible setting for the scene.

It was suggested that *The Long and the Short and the Tall* might be brought to life either by a 'live' dramatic performance in the classroom or by a tape-recorded broadcast performance. You may think that, as the *Luther* scene is concerned with a clash of ideas and not so much with physical action, the tape-recording method might be better as the actors and listeners would have nothing to distract their attention from the spoken word. On the other hand, you may decide that the clash of personality would have more impact if you could see the faces and movements of the characters.

In either case, you should experiment with different people try-ing different parts until you feel that you have the best combination.

Whichever method you use, or whether you decide to experiment with ideas of your own in order to 'lift' the scene from the printed page and bring it to life, it would be helpful to have an introduc-tion. Those especially interested in history in your group might do some research in order to describe the situation in Germany at the beginning of the play, and then you could hear what they have written in order to decide which introduction was the most suitable. It could be written either as a piece of 'straight' narration, or could be spoken in the character of a monk, for example.

When acting the scene, it is important to achieve strong contrast between the voices of the characters. What sorts of voices would you imagine the three characters to have? Don't let the speeches sink into a dreary monotone, especially if you are recording it.

There are opportunities for sound effects here. You may think it a good idea to find out something about mediaeval church singing and use some music at the beginning and end of the scene.

D

Criticism

In any critical discussion that follows the scene, ask yourselves:
1 *Did the arguments, as spoken by the actors, come over clearly?*
2 *Did the characters react to one another, or was each one simply acting by himself, 'in a vacuum'?*
3 *Was it all spoken at the same rate?*
4 *Did you get lines spoken very quickly at times, the way people really speak when they are arguing?*
5 *Which were the most interesting parts of the scene? Why?*
6 *Which character, if any, in this scene do you think John Osborne intended to be the most convincing?*
7 *Which character convinced most by his argument those who were listening to the scene?*

Follow-up

When you have read, discussed and acted the scene, try to think of a situation which could happen today in which three different characters hammer out their ideas. You would have to think first of a strong subject about which people feel deeply. For example:
1 *You could take the problem of racial prejudice. One of the characters could be in favour of racial discrimination and possibly in a position of power. Another could be a young reformer, possibly a student who is against it. The third could be against the student mainly because he dislikes him as a person.*
2 *You could make the scene a town council meeting where people were strongly divided in opinion about what part of the town a proposed new motorway should cut through. More than three characters would be needed for this one.*
3 *The scene could be a meeting in a hospital. A brilliant surgeon is trying to perfect an operating technique to save human lives, based on what he has found out by experimenting with live animals. He asks a young colleague to assist him in further experiments, but the younger man refuses because he says that these experiments are against his principles. If you have a mixed group, the discussion could take place outside the hospital and the wives of both men could enter into the argument.*

From improvisation of any of these scenes, you might work towards a scripted play of your own. I hope you will feel interested enough in the scene from *Luther* to read the whole play.

Billy Liar

Keith Waterhouse and Willis Hall

Billy Liar is the story of a boy with a vivid imagination fighting to escape from a dull background. There are many bored and dissatisfied people in the world today; some are bored by their jobs, some by their surroundings, some by a combination of both. You may have come across people with this 'couldn't care less' attitude to the world around them. However, their boredom is not always caused by dull, routine work or uninteresting family life. It may be the result of some deficiency in themselves: some people would be bored in any job, in any surroundings. They create their own boredom around them, wearing it like a kind of insulating suit between them and the outside world. Such people may never make anything of their lives As Cassius told Brutus in Julius Caesar:

> The fault, dear Brutus, is not in our stars,
> But in ourselves, that we are underlings.

We cannot have much sympathy with people who have the advantage of interesting work and stimulating family background and who remain apathetic and disinterested in life. On the other hand, we can feel some sympathy for Billy Fisher, the central character of Keith Waterhouse and Willis Hall's play *Billy Liar* because his family *is* dull, complacent and lacking in understanding. His boredom and desire to escape are understandable even if they take extreme forms. In order to escape from his drab surroundings Billy invents a fantasy world of his own, full of dramatic incident. We all day-dream from time to time about what we would do if we suddenly became rich, famous or powerful, but Billy day-dreams to such an extent that he lives almost more in his dream-world than in the everyday world around him.

In the scene that follows you will meet Billy himself, Florence, his grandmother, Alice, his mother and Geoffrey, his father. As you read the scene through for the first time, even if it is a silent reading, you will notice how very naturally the dialogue – the lines people speak – flows along. These authors have a quick ear for everyday speech and when you come to read the excerpt aloud, you will find that this natural dialogue helps you to bring the characters to life.

The play is set in an industrial town in the north of England today. Those of you who do not live in the north and do not know the appropriate accent for the characters should resist the temptation to use 'ee bah goom' – North Country comedians' voices. It is safer merely to suggest the accent by broadening the vowel sounds. Then the scene will not turn into a caricature of how real people speak.

From the play

The set consists of a living-room, entrance hall and a section of the garden of GEOFFREY FISHER'S *house. It is a typical lower middle-class detached house in an industrial town in the north of England. To the left of the stage is the garden containing a small garden seat. The entrance to the house from the garden leads directly into the hallway with stairs going up to the bedrooms. Through the hallway is the living-room where most of the action of the play takes place. There is also a door in the living-room R., leading into the kitchen. The room is furnished with an uncut moquette three-piece suite and a dining-room suite in dark oak. The furniture is quite new, but in dreadful taste – as are also the plaster ornaments and the wall plaques with which the room is over-dressed. Above the fireplace is the usual collection of family photographs on the mantelpiece and above the mantelpiece is a large brass-studded circular mirror. The room also contains a cheap and flashy cocktail cabinet, a large television set and also a sideboard with two cupboards.*

As the curtain rises we discover FLORENCE BOOTHROYD *sitting on the couch. She is* ALICE FISHER'S *mother, an old lady in her eighties, who finds it impossible to accustom herself to the modern way of life. She continually talks to herself and when she cannot be heard her lips continue to move. She is in the habit of addressing her remarks to inanimate objects. At the moment she is going through the contents of her large handbag. The handbag is open on her knee and as she takes out each object she examines it and then puts it down on the couch beside her, making a neat display. She has already taken out a few odd possessions and, at the moment, she is holding her old-age pension book. She addresses the sideboard.*

FLORENCE I don't know . . . They haven't stamped my book now . . . They haven't sent it up. It should have gone up last week but they haven't sent it up. (*She puts down the pension book and takes a white hospital appointment card from her handbag.*) That's not right, either. Doctor Blakemore? I've never seen Doctor Blakemore. Which is Doctor Blakemore? I bet it's that blackie. Else it's the lady doctor. I'm not seeing her. Tuesday? They know I never go on Tuesdays. I've never been on Tuesday yet. Doctor Thorpe said . . .

(*It comes to her that she is alone in the room. Putting down the handbag she rises and crosses slowly and flat-footed to the sideboard. She attempts to open the right-hand cupboard but, discovering it is locked, returns to the couch and again takes up her handbag.*) He's as bad. And she encourages him. He lives in that bed. (*Noting the appointment card on the couch she picks it up.*) And where's that crêpe bandage they were going to get me? (*She puts down the card.*) What's he always keep it locked up for, anyroad? There's neither sense nor reason in that. And she never tells you anything.

(ALICE FISHER, GEOFFREY'S *wife, enters from the kitchen. She is a woman in her middle forties. Both* ALICE *and her husband have had working class upbringings, but* GEOFFREY'S *success as a garage owner has moved them up into this new stratum of society. At the moment* ALICE *is caught up in the normal day-to-day rush of breakfast-time. She is speaking to her husband who is in the kitchen.*)

ALICE Well, you do what you think fit, Geoffrey. Do what you like – it's no good my saying anything. But I know what I'd do. He still owes you for that last job you did for him. (ALICE *crosses the room towards the hall, ignoring her mother who speaks to her as she passes.*)

FLORENCE Who's Doctor Blakemore? Which one is that, then? Is that the one you went to?

ALICE (*entering the hall she calls up the stairs*) It's time we were having you down, my lad. That bedroom clock's not fast, you know. It's half-past nine turned. (*She turns and re-enters the living-room.*)

FLORENCE I'll bet it's that blackie, isn't it? I'll bet it's him.

ALICE Who? Blakemore? Yes, I think it is.

FLORENCE I'm not seeing him. I shan't go. I shall stop at home.

ALICE If they say you've got to see him – you've got to see him, mother. It's no good arguing. That's all there is to it.

(GEOFFREY FISHER *enters from the kitchen. He is a tall man in his early fifties. He is carrying a few invoices and, crossing and seating himself in an armchair, he begins to go through them.*)

FLORENCE They caused all that bother on the buses in Birming-

ham. And Egypt. Mau-Mau. I make no wonder Eden's
always so badly. And him upstairs. He's just as bad. I
think it's time his father talked to him. I don't know
why he puts up with it. I can't understand why he lets
him carry on like that.

GEOFFREY (*looking up from the invoices he speaks to* ALICE) It's all
right you talking, Alice, you don't understand. I've got
no choice. I can't turn work away.

ALICE I've said what I've got to say. I'm not saying anything.
I'm keeping out of it.

FLORENCE They let him carry on just as he likes. I wouldn't. I'd
see to him.

GEOFFREY Where's his lordship, then?

FLORENCE I'd tell her. She lets him lead her on. She wants to go
up to him with a wet dish-cloth and wring it over his
face. That'll get him up.

GEOFFREY He wants a good hiding.

FLORENCE . . . that'd move him . . .

ALICE I've shouted him three times.

FLORENCE . . . that'd shift him . . .

GEOFFREY It's every morning alike.

FLORENCE . . . he'd have to get up then.

GEOFFREY You let him do just as he likes!

ALICE (*taking up the poker and a small shovel from the fireplace she crosses into the hall and calls up the stairs*)
Billy! . . . Billy! (*She bangs the poker against the
shovel.*) I shan't tell you again. If I come up there you'll
know about it! I suppose you know what time it is!
Your boiled egg's stone cold and I'm not cooking
another.

FLORENCE She lets him do just as he likes.

GEOFFREY Go up to him. Go up and kick him out. He's idle!
(ALICE *returns into the living-room and places the poker
and shovel back into the fireplace.*)

ALICE It's all right you sitting there. You don't stand need to
talk. You haven't emptied them ashes yet.

FLORENCE She wants to go up to him. I would. (*She is now return-
ing the objects to her handbag and pauses when she
comes to the appointment card.*) It's a mystery to me
about that crêpe bandage. I know I had it. It's in this
house somewhere.

GEOFFREY You can't put anything down in this house. Not without

somebody shifting it. And who keeps taking my invoices
out of that vase? Somebody does.

FLORENCE He ought to see that window's properly locked every
night. He never bolts that back door properly. It wants
doing. There's some more blackies moved in where
Whitakers used to live.

(BILLY FISHER *begins to come down the bedroom stairs.
He is nineteen years old and slightly built. He is wearing an old raincoat over his pyjamas. He is smoking a
cigarette.*)

ALICE Is that him? He's stirred himself at last, then. I'll see
what his breakfast is doing.

(ALICE *goes out to the kitchen as* BILLY *reaches the foot
of the stairs.* BILLY *takes the morning paper from behind
the door and enters the living-room.*)

FLORENCE She lets him do just as he likes.

BILLY (*reading aloud from the paper*) Cabinet Changes Imminent.

GEOFFREY Yes, and you'll be imminent if you don't start getting
up on a morning.

BILLY Good morning, Father.

GEOFFREY Never mind good morning. It's afternoon more like. If
you think your mother's got nothing better to do than
go round cooking six breakfasts every morning you've
got another think coming.

FLORENCE She lets him do what he wants.

BILLY (*ignoring his father he turns and bows, acting out the
situation to his grandmother*) Your servant, ma'am.

GEOFFREY And you stop that game. I'm talking to you. You're
hopeless. And you can start getting dressed before you
come down in the morning.

FLORENCE He wants to burn that raincoat. He wants to burn it.
Sling it on the fire-back. Then he'll have to get dressed
whether or no.

BILLY I gather that he who would burn the raincoat is Father
and he who should get dressed of a morning is my good
self. Why do you always address all your remarks to the
sideboard, Grandmother?

GEOFFREY (*almost rising from his chair*) Here, here, here! Who do
you think you're talking to? You're not out with your
daft mates now. And what time did you get in last
night? If it was night. This morning, more like.

(ALICE *enters from the kitchen.*)

BILLY I really couldn't say. 'Bout half-past eleven, quarter to twelve. Good morning, Mother.

GEOFFREY More like one o'clock, with your half-past eleven! Well, you can start coming in of a night-time. I'm not having you gallivanting round at all hours, not at your age.

BILLY Who are you having gallivanting around, then?

GEOFFREY And I'm not having any of your lip. I'll tell you that, for a start.

ALICE What were you doing down at Foley Bottoms at nine o'clock last night?

BILLY Who says I was down at Foley Bottoms?

ALICE Never mind who says, or who doesn't say. That's got nothing to do with it. You were there – somebody saw you. And it wasn't that Barbara you were with, either.

FLORENCE He wants to make up his mind who he is going with.

GEOFFREY He knocks about with too many lasses. He's out with a different one every night. He's like a lass himself.

BILLY Well, you want to tell whoever saw me to mind their own fizzing business.

ALICE It is our business – and don't you be so cheeky. You're not old enough for that.

FLORENCE If she's coming for her tea this afternoon she wants to tell her. If she doesn't I will.

BILLY I suppose that she who's coming for her tea is Barbara and she who wants to tell her is Mother and . . .

ALICE I've told you – shut up. I'm going to tell her, don't you fret yourself. You've never played fair with that girl. Carrying on. I'm surprised she bothers with you. You shouldn't mess her about like that. One and then the other. That's no way to carry on. I know where you'll finish up – you'll finish up with none of them – that's where you'll finish up.

GEOFFREY He'll finish up on his ear-hole. I'm not having him staying out half the night. Not at his age. He's not old enough. He'll wait till he's twenty-one before he starts them tricks. I've told him before, he can start coming in of a night or else go and live somewhere else.

BILLY Perhaps I will do.

ALICE (*ignoring him*) I can't understand that Barbara – why she does bother with you. Are you supposed to be getting engaged to her or aren't you?

GEOFFREY He doesn't know who he's getting engaged to.

FLORENCE He wants to make his mind up.

ALICE (*ignoring* GEOFFREY *and* FLORENCE) Because she's not like these others, you know. That time I saw you in the arcade with her she looked respectable to me. Not like that Liz or whatever her name is. That scruffy one you reckoned to be going about with. Her in that mucky skirt. Do you ever see anything of her still?

GEOFFREY He sees so many lasses he doesn't know who he does see.

FLORENCE He wants to make his mind up – once and for all. He wants to make his mind up who he is going with.

BILLY I haven't seen Liz for three months.

ALICE Well, who were you with then? Down at Foley Bottoms? Last night?

BILLY Rita.

GEOFFREY Who the hell's Rita?

FLORENCE She wants to see that he makes his mind up.

ALICE I shall tell Barbara this afternoon – I shall tell her, make no mistake about that.

GEOFFREY He's never satisfied with what he has got – that's his trouble. He never has been. It's ever since he left school. It's ever since he took that job – clerking. Clerking for that undertaker – what kind of a job's that?

BILLY Perhaps I might not be doing it much longer.

GEOFFREY You what?

ALICE What do you mean?

BILLY I've been offered a job in London.

GEOFFREY (*turning away in disgust*) Don't talk wet.

ALICE How do you mean? A job in London? What job in London?

BILLY (*taking a crumpled envelope from his raincoat pocket*) What I say, I've been offered a job in London. Script-writing.

GEOFFREY Script-writing.

ALICE What script-writing?

GEOFFREY Script-writing! He can't write his name so you can read it. Who'd set him on?

BILLY (*proudly*) Danny Boon.

ALICE Danny who?

BILLY (*going into a slow, exasperated explanation*) I told you before. Boon. Danny Boon. I told you. He was on at the Empire the week before last. When he was there I told you. I went to see him. I went to his dressing-room. I took him some of my scripts. Well, he's read them. He's read them and he likes them. And he's sent me this letter. He's offered me a job in London. Script-writing. Danny Boon. The comedian. He's been on television.

FLORENCE (*addressing the television*) It's always boxing; boxing and horse shows.

ALICE (*ignoring her*) Danny Boon? I don't remember ever seeing him.

GEOFFREY No, and neither does anybody else. It's another of his tales. Danny Boon! He's made him up.

ALICE What kind of a job?

BILLY I've told you. Script-writing.

GEOFFREY It's like all these other tales he comes home with. He can't say two words to anybody without it's a lie. And what's he been telling that woman in the fish shop about me having my leg off? Do I look as though I've had my leg off?

BILLY It wasn't you. It was Barbara's uncle. She gets everything wrong – that woman in the fish shop.

ALICE You'll have to stop all this making things up, Billy. There's no sense in it at your age. We never know where we are with you. I mean, you're too old for things like that now.

BILLY (*displaying the letter*) Look – all right then. I've got the letter – here. He wants me to go down to see him. In London. To fix things up. I'm going to ring up this morning and give them my notice.

ALICE You can't do things like that, Billy. You can't just go dashing off to London on spec.

GEOFFREY (*disparagingly*) He's not going to no London. It's them that'll be ringing him up, more like. You'll get the sack – I'll tell you what you'll get. What time are you supposed to be going in there this morning, anyroad?

BILLY I'm not. It's my Saturday off this week.

GEOFFREY You said that last week. That's three weeks in a row.

BILLY I got mixed up.

GEOFFREY I've no patience with you. (*He places the invoices in his pocket and rises from his chair.*) Anyway, I've got some work to do if you haven't.

ALICE Are you going in towards town, Geoffrey?

GEOFFREY I'm going in that direction.

ALICE You can drop me off. I'm going down as far as the shops.

GEOFFREY I can if you're not going to be all day getting ready. I'm late now.

ALICE (*crossing towards the hall*) I'm ready now. I've only to slip my coat on.

(ALICE *goes out into the hall and puts on a coat which is hanging on the rack.* GEOFFREY *turns to* BILLY.)

GEOFFREY And you get your mucky self washed – and get dressed. And keep your hands off my razor else you'll know about it.

FLORENCE (*raising her voice*) Is she going past Driver's? Cause there's that pork pie to pick up for this afternoon's tea.

ALICE (*re-entering the living-room*) I'm ready. I'll call in for that pie. (*To* BILLY.) Your breakfast's on the kitchen table. It'll be clap-cold by now.

GEOFFREY (*crossing towards the door. He turns for a final sally at* BILLY) And you can wash them pots up when you've finished. Don't leave it all for your mother.

ALICE I shan't be above an hour, Mother.

(ALICE *and* GEOFFREY *go out through the hall and into the garden.* BILLY *goes into the kitchen.*)

FLORENCE I shouldn't be left on my own. She's not said anything now about the insurance man. I don't know what to give him if he comes.

(ALICE *and* GEOFFREY *are moving down the garden.*)

GEOFFREY I'm only going as far as the lane, you know. I don't know why you can't get the bus.

(ALICE *and* GEOFFREY *go off.* BILLY *re-enters from the kitchen. He is carrying a cup and a teapot.*)

BILLY I can't eat that egg. It's stone cold.

FLORENCE There's too much waste in this house. It's all goodness just thrown down the sink. We had it to eat. When I was his age we couldn't leave nothing. If we didn't eat it then it was put out the next meal. When we had eggs, that was. We were lucky to get them. You had to make do with what there was. Bread and dripping.

BILLY (*sitting down he pours himself a cup of tea*) Do you want a cup of tea?

FLORENCE And if you weren't down at six o'clock of a morning you didn't get that.

BILLY (*he drinks and grimaces*) They don't drink tea in London at this time of a morning. It's all coffee. That's what I'll be doing this time next week.

FLORENCE Sundays was just the same. No lying-in then.

(BILLY *and his grandmother are now in their own separate dream-worlds.*)

BILLY Sitting in a coffee-bar. Espresso. With a girl. Art student. Duffel-coat and dirty toe nails. I discovered her the night before. Contemplating suicide.

FLORENCE If you had a job in them days you had to stick to it. You couldn't get another.

BILLY (*addressing his imaginary companion*) Nothing is as bad as it seems, my dear. Less than a week ago my father felt the same as you. Suicidal. He came round after the operation and looked down where his legs should have been. Nothing.

FLORENCE We couldn't go traipsing off to London or anywhere else. If we got as far as Scarborough we were lucky.

BILLY Just an empty space in the bed. Well, he'll never be World Champion now. A broken man on two tin legs.

(BILLY *slowly levers himself out of his chair and limps slowly and painfully around the room leaning heavily against the furniture.*)

FLORENCE (*addressing* BILLY *in the third person*) He's not right in the head.

(BILLY *realizes he is being watched and comes out of his fantasy.*)

I wouldn't care, but it makes me poorly watching him.

BILLY (*rubbing his leg and by way of explanation*) Cramp.

Understanding the play

Characters

FLORENCE BOOTHROYD: You will find a description of her in the stage directions at the beginning of the play. Remember that although she appears to talk to herself all the time, her actual speeches must be heard. She is not completely cut off from the rest of the family and probably hears a great deal more than she seems to.

ALICE FISHER: Billy's mother is the centre of the family and the others' arguments revolve round her. Although she is set in her ideas, unimaginative and superficial in outlook, she is a strong woman in her way.

GEOFFREY FISHER: Billy's father. Although he bulldozes his way through the scene and gets at Billy continuously, there is more to the character than mere bluster. In the second act there is a scene in which he tries to get through to Billy, so don't make Geoffrey completely bad-tempered: his bark may be worse than his bite.

BILLY FISHER: He is nineteen. Although he is so different from his family, he is still a part of it with the same accent and mannerisms. He is not a freak, nor a figure of fun and never just a liar. Although many of his lines are funny, there is something pathetic about him. He has much more imagination and a quicker brain than the others. However, at the very end of the play, we see that he hasn't the courage to put his dreams of escaping from his environment into practice, when, after packing his suitcase and leaving to catch the midnight train to London in order to take a job, he unexpectedly returns slowly and dejectedly. He comes into the living-room, switches on the radio, begins to unpack his suitcase. As the music from a dance band swells up, he automatically starts to conduct. Billy is back in his dream world again.

How the playwright handles dialogue

If you have ever tried to write a play yourself, you will know how difficult it is to make the characters speak like themselves and not like you. It takes an experienced writer to make each character speak in an individual way. The dialogue of a play shows at once the professionalism, or otherwise, of the writer and whether he has an ear for the way in which different people express themselves and whether he can write in natural speech idiom.

An amateur playwright I knew once decided to try to get his dialogue from real life. He switched on a tape recorder and recorded a group of people talking when they didn't realize what was happening. Afterwards he played back their conversation. Alas for his hopes of getting anything useful for his play. The recorded conversation was a muddle of repetitions, unfinished sentences and dull remarks. Sometimes there was an empty silence with no one saying anything; sometimes there was a babel of noise with three or four people speaking at the same time.

A dramatist has to select what his characters say: to try to reproduce real life conversation is useless.

Shakespeare said that the function of acting 'is to hold, as 'twere, the mirror up to nature', and this mirror is the actor's ability to show human beings on the stage. The remark applies to play writing, too, but in this case, the mirror is the playwright's mind. It is no good showing just 'nature' and how people speak and behave in real life; he has to give an impression or reflection of their talk and action at its most interesting and significant.

Read through the scene again and ask yourselves these questions about the dialogue:

1 How do the playwrights give you an immediate impression of Florence's rambling mind in her first speech?
2 How many repetitions can you find in it?
3 Alice's sentences are much shorter than Florence's. Why do you think the playwrights have written her lines like this?
4 In the scene just before Billy comes on, the give-and-take of family life conversation is vividly illustrated: the sudden arguments, the way everyone's words sometimes overlap and no one listens to anyone else, the way everyone will suddenly turn on one member of the family. Can you find a series of speeches that do this?
5 How do the dramatists suggest Billy's character in his first few lines of dialogue?
6 Billy obviously gets on his father's nerves. Can you find some of the things that Billy says that particularly annoy Geoffrey?
7 What does Geoffrey say that you think is particularly likely to annoy Billy?
8 How does Billy's way of expressing himself differ from the rest of the family's?

9 After his parents have gone, Billy has a scene with his grand-mother in which each is living in a separate dream-world. How does each one's line of thought develop?
10 What finally makes Florence take notice of Billy?
11 Why do you think the playwrights give Billy only one word of explanation as to what he is doing?
12 Do you think this is more effective than a long sentence would have been?

Bringing the play to life

As this scene is at the beginning of the play, it needs no introduction, and you will find that the episode is complete in itself. After reading it through two or three times, it would be helpful to improvise a scene of your own, using the whole group, or two or three smaller ones. The situation that you start from could be very like the one in the play, a number of people in a family coming down to breakfast at different times and some having to go off to work, or to school, others staying behind for different reasons. It would be easier, if your numbers are large, to divide into three or four small groups and let each work out an improvised scene. Although you all start with the same central situation, you will find out that the dialogue which you make up as you go along will be quite different in each group. After some time working separately in groups, you should watch what each one has improvised, in turn. In this way you will see how everyday speech repeats itself, is hesitant, full of searchings for words and unfinished sentences. You will notice that sometimes everyone is silent at the same moment and at others that there is a sudden jumble of sound with several people speaking at once. However, you may create a piece of dialogue that flows along quite naturally and effectively. These are the lines that you would keep if you were working towards a scripted play of your own based on your improvised scene. This type of improvisation is helpful because, by doing it, you realize how much shaping and selecting of everyday speech has to be done by playwrights before an interesting play emerges.

After some time spent in improvisation, you will be ready to tackle the scene itself. Again it may be acted as if for a stage performance or you may decide to record it. If you use more than one group, each would watch and listen to the other's final effort.

Criticism

In the discussion that should follow the performance in the classroom, pay particular attention to the way that the lines have been spoken. Some people can 'lift' written dialogue from the page and give it the sound of natural, unrehearsed speech quite easily. The lines appear to come into the speaker's head just at the moment

E

that he is saying them. Others find this difficult to do and very often their lines sound stilted, unnatural, like audible print. One must try to get one's mind behind the words and mean and feel them in order to make them convincing.

Follow-up

I hope that this scene will have made you aware of the value of natural, vivid dialogue. It may help you to listen critically to the dialogue you hear in television plays, documentaries, films, stage plays and even commercials.

Always ask yourselves:

1 Would this kind of person speak like this?
2 Would they know the kinds of words that the playwright or scriptwriter has given them to say?
3 Even if they knew the words, would they be likely to choose them?
4 Do the various characters sound like themselves, or are they speaking with the writer's own voice all the time?

We tend to accept entertainment uncritically these days. You may be surprised at the number of shocks you get if you listen to scripted words with a critical ear.

Here are some suggested situations; try to write snatches of dialogue for them.

1 One half of the family wants to watch a sports programme on television; the other half is anxious to see a documentary. The programmes are on different channels and the times clash. Start your dialogue two minutes before each programme is due to begin.
2 The family returns from an evening out to find that the house has been burgled. Someone forgot to lock up; but which one was it?
3 Two of you are walking along the road. A stranger asks you the way to a certain not very well known street. You think you know the way; your companion thinks differently. Make up the dialogue.

Some of you may be sufficiently interested to write a complete play of your own. But remember that the test of dramatic dialogue is what it sounds like when spoken by the actor.

Roots

Arnold Wesker

This play is about the problem of communication between people; about the power of words to bridge the gaps between them and to help them to understand one another.

The word *communication* is used a great deal nowadays, when we describe people's relationships with one another. What does it mean exactly? When two people are able to communicate with each other, they are able to put their feelings and ideas into words in such a way that each understands the other. It is a two-way process. Each is 'tuned-in' to the other's wavelength. Sometimes, when two people know each other very well, they are able to communicate with each other – to know what the other is thinking – without actual words.

Roots is set in Norfolk, in a farm labouring community. Beatie Bryant has come home to her family for a holiday. While working as a waitress, she has met a young man who is deeply interested in the arts and politics, and he has opened her eyes to the power of language. Now she wants to pass on all her new interests – in words, in books, in painting, in music – to her stolid and unimaginative family, who are so inarticulate that they cannot even find the words to deal with a family crisis when it arises in the final scene of the play.

In the first excerpt given here, we see the failure in communication between Beatie and her mother, Mrs Bryant. Each drives along her own line of thought and at no point do the two people meet in understanding. They are isolated from each other. All that Mrs Bryant can say about her daughter's paintings is: 'Good colours, ent they?' Beatie sings a folk song; her mother shows enthusiasm for a cheap pop song. There is no point of contact between them.

In the final scene, Ronnie, the young man who has influenced her so much, is expected for tea to meet the whole of Beatie's family. Mrs Bryant has prepared a mammoth trifle and the menfolk are dressed uncomfortably in their best clothes. At the moment when the second excerpt starts, there is a knock on the door and the postman delivers a letter. It is from Ronnie, telling Beatie that

he and she have no future together. Mrs Bryant turns on Beatie
and taunts her with all that Beatie has been doing to try to inject
life into her family, to raise their standards; when all the time
Beatie herself is no better than the rest of them: 'It turn out she
do just the same things she say I do.'

Beatie listens despairingly at first; then slowly she starts speaking.
Gradually the words begin to flow, and the play ends on a note of
exultation as Beatie finds herself at last articulate – able to think, to
experience and to express what she thinks and feels.

From the play

The scene is the kitchen in the home of BEATIE BRYANT'S *parents, a cottage in a Norfolk village.* BEATIE *has come home for a visit after three years working in London.*

BEATIE Mother! Did I write and tell you I've took up painting? I started five months ago. Working in gouache. Ronnie says I'm good. Says I should carry on and maybe I can sell them for curtain designs. 'Paint, girl' he say. 'Paint! The world is full of people who don't do the things they want, so you paint and give us all hope!'
(MRS BRYANT *enters.* BEATIE *shows her the paintings.*)
Like 'em?

MRS BRYANT (*looks at them a second*) Good colours, ent they? (*She is unmoved.* BEATIE *returns paintings to other room.*) Yes gal, I ent got no row wi' Pearl but I ask her to change my Labour Tote man 'cos I wanted to give the commission to Charlie Gorleston and she didn't do it. Well, if she can be like that I can be like that, too. You gonna do some baking you say?

BEATIE (*enters from front room putting on pinafore and carrying a parcel*) Right now. Here y'are, Daphne Bryant, present for you. I want eggs, flour, sugar and marg. I'm gonna bake a sponge and give it frilling. (*Goes to larder to collect things.*)

MRS BRYANT (*unpacking parcel. It is a pinafore*) We both got one now.
(MRS BRYANT *goes to sink to peel potatoes as* BEATIE *at table proceeds to separate four eggs, the yolk of which she starts whipping with sugar. She sings meanwhile a ringing folk song.*)

BEATIE Oh a dialogue I'll sing you as true as me life
Between a coal owner and poor pitman's wife.
As she were a walking along the highway
She met a coal owner and to him did say,
'Derry down, down, down Derry down.'
Whip the eggs till they're light yellow, he says.

MRS BRYANT Who says?

BEATIE Ronnie.
'Good morning, Lord Firedamp,' the good woman said,

'I'll do you no harm, sir, so don't be afraid.
If you'd been where I'd been for most of my life
You wouldn't turn pale at a poor pitman's wife.'
Singing down, down, down Derry down.

MRS BRYANT What song's that?

BEATIE A coalmining song.

MRS BRYANT I tell you what I reckon's a good song, that 'I'll wait for you in the heaven's blue'. I reckon that's a lovely song. I do. Jimmy Samson he sing that.

BEATIE It's like twenty other songs, it don't mean anything and it's sloshy and sickly.

MRS BRYANT Yes, I reckon that's a good song, that.

BEATIE (suddenly crossing to MRS BRYANT) Listen, Mother, let me see if I can explain something to you. Ronnie always say that's the point of knowing people. 'It's no good having friends who scratch each other's back,' he say. 'The excitement in knowing people is to hand on what you know and to learn what you don't know. Learn from me,' he say, 'I don't know much but learn what I know.' So let me try and explain to you what he explain to me.

MRS BRYANT (on hearing a bus) There go the half past eleven bus to Diss – blust, that's early. (Puts potatoes in saucepan on oven and goes to collect runner beans which she prepares.)

BEATIE (following her around) Mother, I'm talking to you. Blust, woman, it's not often we get together and really talk, it's nearly always me listening to you telling who's dead. Just listen a second.

MRS BRYANT (back at sink) Well go on, gal, but you always take so long to say it.

BEATIE What are the words of that song?

MRS BRYANT I don't know all the words.

BEATIE I'll tell you. (Recites them.)
I'll wait for you in the heaven's blue
As my arms are waiting now.
Please come to me and I'll be true
My love shall not turn sour.
I hunger, I hunger, I cannot wait longer,
My love shall not turn sour.
There! Now what do that mean!

MRS BRYANT (surprised) Well, don't you know what that mean?

BEATIE (moving to her mother again) I mean what do they do

to you? How do the words affect you? Are you moved?
Do you find them beautiful?

MRS BRYANT Them's as good words as any.

BEATIE But do they make you feel better?

MRS BRYANT Blust gal! Them ent supposed to be a laxative!

BEATIE I must be mad to talk with you.

(*Two weeks have passed. It is Saturday, the day* RONNIE
is to arrive. On the table is a spread of food.)
(*There is a knock on the front door.*)

BEATIE He's here, he's here! (*She goes off* U.L. *but it is only
the postman and she returns with a letter and a parcel.*)
Oh the fool, the silly fool. Trust him to write a letter on
the day he's coming. Parcel for you, Mother.

PEARL Oh, that'll be your dress from the club.

MRS BRYANT What dress is this, then? I didn't ask for no dress from
the club.

PEARL Yes, you did, you did ask me, didn't she ask me, Frank?
Why, we were looking through the book together,
Mother.

MRS BRYANT No matters what we was doin' together, I aren't hevin'
it.

PEARL But, Mother, you distinctly –

MRS BRYANT I aren't hevin' it so there now!

(BEATIE *has read the letter – the contents stun her and
she gasps, bringing her hand to her mouth. She cannot
move. She stares around speechlessly at everyone.*)
Well, what's the matter wi' you, gal? Let's have a read.
(*Takes letter and reads contents in a dead flat but loud
voice – as though it were a proclamation.*) 'My dear
Beatie. It wouldn't really work, would it? My ideas
about handing on a new kind of life to people are quite
useless and romantic if I'm really honest. Perhaps I am
asking too much of you. If I were a healthy human
being it might have been all right but most of us intel-
lectuals are pretty sick and neurotic – as you have often
observed – and we couldn't build a world even if we
were given the reins of government – not yet, any rate.
This is depressing, and I just don't know what went
wrong. I don't blame you for being stubborn, I don't

blame you for ignoring every suggestion I ever made –
I only blame myself for encouraging you to believe we
could make a go of it. We've had precious moments
together. But now two weeks of your not being here has
given me the cowardly chance to think about it and
decide and I –'

BEATIE (*screaming and snatching letter*) Shut up!

MRS BRYANT Oh – so we know now, do we?

MR BRYANT What's this then – ent he comin'?

MRS BRYANT Yes, we know now.

MR BRYANT Ent he comin', I ask?

BEATIE (*shouting*) No, he ent comin'.

(*An awful silence ensues. Everyone looks uncomfortable.*)

JENNY (*softly*) Well blust, gal, didn't you know this was going to
happen?

(BEATIE *shakes her head.*)

MRS BRYANT So we're stubborn, are we?

JENNY Shut you up, Mother, the girl's upset.

MRS BRYANT Well I can see that, I can see that, he ent coming, I can
see that, and we're here like bloody fools, I can see that.

PEARL Well, did you quarrel all that much, Beatie?

BEATIE (*as if discovering this for the first time*) He always wanted
me to help him but I never could. Once he tried to
teach me to type but soon ever I made a mistake I'd
give up. I'd give up every time! I couldn't bear making
mistakes. I don't know why but I couldn't bear making
mistakes.

MRS BRYANT Oh – so we're hearin' the other side o' the story now, are
we?

BEATIE He used to suggest I start to copy real objects on to my
paintings instead of only abstracts and I never took heed.

MRS BRYANT Oh, so you never took heed.

JENNY Shut you up, I say.

BEATIE He gimme a book sometimes and I never bothered to
read it.

FRANK (*not maliciously*) What about all this discussion we
heard of?

BEATIE I never discussed things. He used to beg me to discuss
things but I never saw the point on it.

PEARL And he got riled because o' that?

BEATIE (*trying to understand*) I didn't have any patience.

MRS BRYANT Now it's coming out.

BEATIE I couldn't help him – I never knew patience. Once he looked at me with terrified eyes and said 'we've been together for three years but you don't know who I am or what I'm trying to say – and you don't care, do you?'

MRS BRYANT And there she was tellin' me.

BEATIE I never knew what he wanted – I didn't think it mattered.

MR BRYANT And there she were gettin' us to solve that moral problem and now we know she didn't even do it herself. That's a rum un, ent it?

MRS BRYANT The apple don't fall far from the tree – that it don't.

BEATIE (*wearily*) So you're proud on it? You sit there smug and you're proud that a daughter of yours wasn't able to help her boy friend? Look at you. All of you. You can't say anything. You can't even help your own flesh and blood. Your daughter's bin ditched. It's your problem as well, isn't it? I'm part of your family, aren't I? Well, help me then! Give me words of comfort! Talk to me – for God's sake, someone, talk to me. (*She moves away* U.S. *and cries at last.*)

MR BRYANT Well, what do we do now?

MRS BRYANT (*rising*) We sit down and we eat, that's what we do now.

JENNY Don't be soft, Mother, we can't leave the girl crying like that.

MRS BRYANT (*standing behind her chair*) Well, blust, 't'ent my fault she's cryin'. I did what I could – I prepared all this food, I'd've treated him as my own son if he'd come but he heven't! We got a whole family gathering specially to greet him, all on us, look, but he heven't come. So what am I supposed to do?

BEATIE (*moving quickly to* MRS BRYANT) My God, Mother, I hate you – the only thing I ever wanted and I weren't able to keep him, I didn't know how. I hate you, I hate . . .

(MRS BRYANT *slaps* BEATIE'S *face. Everyone is a little shocked at this harsh treatment.*)

MRS BRYANT There! I hed enough!

MR BRYANT Well, what d'you wanna do that for?

MRS BRYANT I hed enough. All this time she've bin home she've bin tellin' me I didn't do this and I didn't do that and I heven't understood half what she've said and I've hed enough. She talk about bein' part o' the family but she've never lived at home since she've left school, look. Then she go away from here and fill her head wi' high class squit and then it turn out she don't understand any on it herself. It turn out she do just the same things she say I do. (*Into* BEATIE's *face*.) Well, am I right, gal? I'm right, ent I? When you tell me I was stubborn, what you mean was that he told you you was stubborn – eh? When you tell me I don't understand you mean you don't understand, isn't it? When you tell me I don't make no effort you mean you don't make no effort. Well, what you blaming me for? Blaming me all the time! I haven't bin responsible for you since you left home – you bin on your own. All right, so I am a bloody fool – all right! So I know it! A whole two weeks I've bin told it. Well, so then I can't help you, my gal, no that I can't, and you get used to that once and for all.

BEATIE No you can't, Mother, I know you can't.

MRS BRYANT I suppose doin' all those things for him weren't enough. I suppose he weren't satisfied wi' goodness only.

BEATIE Oh, what's the use?

MRS BRYANT Well, don't you sit there an' sigh, gal, like you was Lady Nevershit. I ask you something. Answer me. You do the talking then. Go on – you say you know something we don't so you do the talking. Talk – go on, talk gal.

BEATIE (*to door* U.R., *despairingly*) I can't, Mother, you're right – the apple don't fall far from the tree, do it? You're right, I'm like you. Stubborn, empty, wi' no tools for livin'. I got no roots in nothing. I come from a family o' farm labourers yet I ent got no roots – just like town people – just a mass o' nothin'.

FRANK Roots, gal? What do you mean, roots?

BEATIE (*quickly down to* R. *of* FRANK, *impatiently*) Roots, roots, roots! Hell, Frankie, you're in the fields all day, you should know about growing things. Roots! The things you come from, the things that feed you. The things that make you proud of yourself—roots!

MR BRYANT You got a family, ent you?

BEATIE I am not talking about family roots – I mean – the – I mean – Look! Ever since it begun the world's bin growin', hasn't it? Things hev happened, things have bin discovered, people have bin thinking and improving and inventing but what do we know about it all?

JIMMY   What is she on about?

(There are various interjections from all.)

BEATIE What do you mean what am I on about? I'm talking!
Listen to me! *(The noise fades and slowly the words
begin to flow.)* I'm tellin' you that the world's bin growing for two thousand years and we heven't noticed it.
I'm telling you that we don't know what we are or
where we come from. I'm telling you something's cut
us off from the beginning. I'm telling you we've got no
roots. Blimey Joe! We've all got large allotments, we
all grow things around us so we should know about
roots. You know how to keep your flowers alive, don't
you, Mother? Jimmy – you know how to keep the roots
of your vegies strong and healthy. It's not only the corn
that need strong roots, you know, it's us too. But what've
we got? Go on, tell me, what've we got? We don't know
where we push up from and we don't bother neither.

PEARL   Well, I aren't grumblin'.

BEATIE You say you aren't – oh yes, you say so, but look at you.
What've you done since you come in? Hev you said
anythin'? I mean really said or done anything to show
you're alive? Alive! Blust, what do it mean? Do you
know what it means? Any of you? Shall I tell you what
Susie said when I went and saw her? She say she don't
care if that ole atom bomb drop and she die – that's
what she say. And you know why she say it? I'll tell you
why, because if she had to care she'd have to do something about it and she find that too much effort. Yes she
do. She can't be bothered – she's too bored with it all.
That's what we all are – we're all too bored.

MRS BRYANT Blust, woman – bored you say, bored? You say Susie's
bored, with a radio and television an' that? I go t'hell if
she's bored!

BEATIE Oh yes, we turn on a radio or a TV set maybe, or we go
to the pictures – if them's love stories or gangsters – but
isn't that the easiest way out? Anything so long as we
don't have to make an effort. Well, am I right? You
know I'm right. Education ent only books and music –
it's asking questions, all the time. There are millions of
us, all over the country and no one, not one of us, is
asking questions, we're all taking the easiest way out.
Everyone I ever worked with took the easiest way out.

We don't fight for anything, we're so mentally lazy we
might as well be dead. Blust, we are dead! And you
know what Ronnie say sometimes? He say it serves
us right! That's what he say – it's our own bloody
fault!

JIMMY So that's us summed up then – so we know where we are
then!

MRS BRYANT Well, if he don't reckon we count for nothin', then it's
as well he didn't come. There! It's as well he didn't
come.

BEATIE Oh, he thinks we count all right – living in mystic com-
munion with nature. Living in mystic bloody commu-
nion with nature, indeed. But us count? Count, Mother.
I wonder. Do we? Do you think we really count? You
don' wanna take any notice of what them ole papers say
about the workers bein' all important these days – that's
all squit! Cos we aren't. Do you think when the really
talented people in the country get to work they get to
work for us? Hell if they do! Do you think they don't
know we 'ont make the effort? The writers don't write
thinkin' we can understand, nor the painters don't paint
expecting us to be interested – that they don't nor don't
the composers give out music thinking we can appreci-
ate it. 'Blust,' they say, 'the masses is too stupid for us to
come down to them. Blust,' they say, 'if they don't make
no effort why should we bother?' So you know who come
along? The slop singers and the pop writers and the
film makers and women's magazines and the Sunday
papers and the picture strip love stories – that's who
come along, and you don't have to make no effort for
them, it come easy. 'We know where the money lie,' they
say, 'hell we do! The workers've got it so let's give them
what they want. If they want slop songs and film idols
we'll give 'em that then. If they want words of one syl-
lable, we'll give 'em that then. If they want the third
rate, blust! We'll give 'em that then. (*Moving* U.S. *with
her back to them.*) Anything's good enough for them
'cos they don't ask for no more!' The whole stinkin'
commercial world insults us and we don't care a damn.
Well, Ronnie's right – it's our own bloody fault. We
want the third rate, we got it! We got it! We got it!
We . . .

(*Suddenly* BEATIE *stops as if listening to herself. She pauses, turns with an ecstatic smile on her face.*)
D'you hear that? D'you hear it? Did you listen to me? I'm talking. Jenny, Frankie, Mother – I'm not quoting no more.

MRS BRYANT (*resuming her seat at table*) Oh hell, I hed enough of her – let her talk a while, she'll soon get fed up.

(*The others join her at the table and proceed to eat and murmur. When they have settled* BEATIE *moves slowly D.S. as though a vision were revealed to her.*)

BEATIE God in heaven, Ronnie! It does work, it's happening to me, I can feel it's happened, I'm beginning, on my own two feet – I'm beginning . . .

(*The murmur of the family at the table grows as* BEATIE'S *last cry is heard. Whatever she will do they will continue to live as before and* BEATIE *stands alone, articulate at last.*)

THE CURTAIN SLOWLY FALLS.

Understanding the play

Characters

Having read the excerpts through a couple of times, you should be ready to talk about the characters, to make up your minds what they are really like. Until you have done this, you will be unable to speak the lines convincingly.

BEATIE: She is twenty-two and differs from the rest of her family not so much because she is cleverer than they are but because she seems to have broken through the boundaries of their narrow world to a wider life.

Re-read the scene between Beatie and her mother and ask your-selves:

1 Which lines show Beatie's enthusiasm and drive?
2 Does Beatie make any attempt to listen to Mrs Bryant's gossip?

MRS BRYANT: She is described by the playwright in these words: 'Mrs Bryant is a short, stout woman of fifty. She spends most of the day on her own and consequently when she has a chance to speak to anybody she says as much as she can as fast as she can. . . . She speaks very loudly all the time so that her friendliest tone sounds aggressive, and she manages to dramatize the smallest piece of gossip into something significant.'

1 Can you find an example of this last trait in her character in the first scene?
2 She says of Beatie in the second act of the play: 'Thank God you come home sometimes, gal – you do bring a little life with you anyway.' However, in the final scene she changes in her attitude to Beatie. What do you think causes this change?
3 What provokes her into slapping Beatie's face?
4 How much do you sympathize with the things that Mrs Bryant says in her speech beginning: 'I hed enough. All this time she've bin home she've bin tellin' me I didn't do this and I didn't do that.'

JENNY: Beatie's sister, married to Jimmy. She is an easy-going type, well settled in the family groove and very friendly.

JIMMY: Jenny's husband. A young garage mechanic, not given to much thought.

Do you think, judging from the remarks he makes in the last scene of the play, that he will ever understand Beatie?

FRANK BRYANT: Beatie's brother. He is described as being 'pleasant and dressed in a blue pin-striped suit. . . . An odd sort of shyness makes him treat everything as a joke.' Like Jimmy, he has very little to say in the scene, but it is important that both of them react to what the other characters say.

Can you make a list of notes for the scene to show what you think Frank's reactions will be to all that is said by the others?

PEARL BRYANT: Frank's wife. She is quite content with her situation in life. Has firm opinions and will probably never change them.

Can you find the speech which gives a clue to her character?

MR BRYANT: Beatie's father. He is a farm labourer. He has just been put on casual labour and half pay and this will affect his attitude in the scene. He is a sick man, described by the playwright as 'small and shrivelled'. He is an insignificant and feckless character.

What do you think his feelings for Beatie are when he sees that she has been rejected by Ronnie?

Using conflict to create interest

One of the essential ingredients of a well-written play is conflict. A good writer gives two sides of an argument and leaves you room to think for yourself and decide which side you have the more sympathy with. You will notice that Mrs Bryant is given the chance to attack Beatie in the second excerpt.

Before acting the scenes, ask yourselves these questions about the writer's use of conflict:

1 *What are Beatie's objections to the type of pop song that Mrs Bryant likes?*

2 *Do you agree with what Beatie says about: 'I'll wait for you in the heaven's blue'?*

3 *Who do you think is the more to blame in the first excerpt for the failure of Beatie and her mother to understand each other's feelings?*

4 *Why do you think that Beatie hates her mother in the final scene of the play?*

5 *Mrs Bryant has a long speech beginning: 'I hed enough. All this time she've bin home . . .' Can you put her arguments against Beatie into your own words?*

6 *Who do you think is to blame for the fact that Ronnie doesn't want to continue knowing Beatie?*

7 *What do you understand by the expression: 'The apple don't fall far from the tree'?*

8 *Do you think that Beatie's outburst at the end of the scene will have any effect on her family?*

9 *Who is Beatie attacking, apart from her family?*

10 *Do you agree with these remarks made by Beatie?*

'*Education ent only books and music – it's asking questions, all the time. There are millions of us, all over the country and no one, not one of us, is asking questions, we're all taking the easiest way out. . . . We don't fight for anything, we're so mentally lazy we might as well be dead.*'

Here are three situations likely to cause family conflicts:

(a) One member has married into a rich family and is now much better off than his or her own people. He or she returns home for a visit.

(b) One member of the family is ambitious and anxious to get on; the others are quite content to jog along as they are. The ambitious one asks for some money to eke out a grant.

(c) The boys in the family are favoured at the expense of the girls. This affects everything from education to household chores.

Can you think of three other situations? Try to improvise scenes around the three given here.

Bringing the play to life

When acting these scenes, you will find great opportunity for team-work, particularly in the second. One of the tests of a good actor is how he listens when other people are talking, and so, although Pearl, Frank, Jenny, Jimmy and Mr Bryant have very little to say themselves, they must listen to the dialogue all the time and react to it. Remember that this is a family crisis.

As preparation for acting the scene, you could divide into two or three groups each representing a family, preferably with a completely different background. It would be interesting to invent a different family crisis for each group and then improvise the scenes round them. For example, the situation could be:

1 The sudden arrival of the police to arrest one of the family.
2 A letter arrives from the father's firm telling him that he has to work overseas.

Whatever the situation that you choose to improvise around, be sure that the characters are distinct and, if possible, get some conflict into the scene. The family could all be united against one member; or split evenly – parents against children, or the sons on the opposite side from the daughters. Choose any combination of forces that you think would be likely in your given crisis.

When you have acted out your improvised scenes, you will be in a better position to tackle the excerpts from *Roots*.

Criticism

After you have acted the two scenes, it would be useful to have a discussion about the performance from two angles:

(*a*) from the point of view of the team-work that was achieved;
(*b*) from the point of view of the way the moments of conflict emerged.

Ask yourselves:

1 How did the people playing the smaller parts listen and react to what Beatie and Mrs Bryant said?

F

2 *Was there sufficient contrast of personality between Beatie and her mother and between Beatie and the rest of the family?*
3 *Did Beatie manage to keep her long speeches interesting?*

Follow-up

If you have been interested by these scenes, you will want to read the whole play. Arnold Wesker is a playwright with strong feelings and interesting ideas; find out what other plays he has written and read those, too.

Beatie's last long speech is about the mass media – films, magazines, newspapers, pop art. She says that the people behind all these things play down to the masses, try to reduce everyone to the lowest common denominator of intelligence. It would be an interesting experiment to take a popular magazine or a pop song and look at it critically to try to find out for yourselves whether you think what Beatie says is true. Is it third rate, and are the editors and composers trying to cash in on current taste, or is it stimulating stuff that makes you think?

Finally, ask yourselves if you could do better. Experiment and see if you can.

The Bespoke Overcoat

Wolf Mankowitz

'Love is a luxury which very poor people can afford, and *The Bespoke Overcoat* is a story of this love.' That is how Wolf Mankowitz introduces his one-act play and it is this thought which underlines all the dialogue. The following three scenes from the play will give you an idea of how he works out his theme.

In this book, we have already seen a group of men facing a common danger, each in his own way; we have seen a man daring to be an individual in the face of the enormous power of the mediaeval church, and two members of unimaginative families striving for betterment. Now let us see how Morry, the poor Jewish tailor, stretches out a hand in friendship to Fender, who is poorer than he is.

In the first scene, Morry tells us that his friend, Fender, is dead. Fender felt the cold bitterly, but was too poor to buy a new overcoat and asked Morry to mend his old one, which was so worn that it was falling to pieces. In the next scene (Scene 4 of the play) we see Morry and Fender discussing the old overcoat. Morry says that it is impossible to mend and promises to make Fender a new one, a bespoke overcoat for ten pounds. Fender is going to save up for it out of his meagre wages as a clerk at Ranting's warehouse. But before he can do this he gets the sack and in Scene 11 we see him dying of cold and starvation.

As the playwright says, the story is a sad one. Fender does not get his bespoke overcoat. We are shown the twinge of conscience that Morry feels because, although he loves Fender, his love has not been able to give him his bespoke overcoat in time; his love has not prevented Fender from dying of malnutrition and cold. Although, in this sense, the story is a sad one, it is also one of great hope and encouragement. We see the comradeship and spirit that can be found in human beings when everything seems to be against them.

From the play

The action of the play is distributed among three separate areas permanently set and used in turn.

Area 'A', midstage R., is RANTING'S *warehouse, which consists of a sizeable table, placed obliquely, with a chair or stool L. and to the U.S. end of it. U.S. of the table, and rather behind it, a large rack supports a selection of overcoats on hangers.*

Area 'B' is D.S.C. and has no furnishing.

Area 'C', midstage L., is MORRY'S *room, which consists of a mattress lying obliquely on the floor, and beside it R., at the U.S. end, a chair.*

These three areas are encompassed by a black surround with entrances D.R., D.L., and U.C. During the entire play, these are in total darkness, as are any two of the acting areas not being used. Throughout, the stage directions will be related to the areas described.

When the curtain rises MORRY *is standing in the area 'B', with a navy blue overcoat over his arm. A barrel organ is playing off, and fades out as the light at 'B' fades in.*

1. MORRY Fender dead. That old man Fender dead. Funny thing. You're a good tailor, he used to say. You're a good tailor. No, you're a good tailor. Look around. I don't care where you look, he says, you are a number one tailor. Look at this coat, he says. What, that old coat? A coat must be twenty years old. Mind you, I can tell straightaway by the cross-stitch it's my coat. It's your coat, he shouts. You made it. Twenty-two years ago I come to you for a coat. This is him. I still got him. You got a good point. I tell him, I'm a good tailor. It's only the truth. I'm a good tailor. Straightaway, I see I made a mistake. I fell in. How much, Fender says, will you take to mend a coat like this? I ask you. It's falling to pieces on his back. I told him straight, no nonsense. Look, Fender, I told him, I can run you up a pair of trousers from lining canvas you can walk up Saville Road nobody can tell you from the Prince of Wales. But, Fender, do me a favour. Take the coat somewhere else. A new coat I can make, but the Union says no miracles. A rag, that's all. I got my clients to think

about. Good afternoon. A lovely piece of worsted. Mind you, I got a suit length here: in a hundred year you wouldn't see nothing better. Clients. Fender dead. An old man. (*Turns U.S., still speaking.*) He sits in that stone cold warehouse all day long. (*Turns head round to audience.*) Who could mend such a coat? (*Moves slowly U.S. to 'C' exit.*) That's enough. (*Light starts to fade.*) Leave me alone. All this nagging, nagging. (*He has gone, and so has the light.*)

2.   (*As the light fades in on 'C' FENDER is standing U.S. of mattress. MORRY enters D.L.*)

MORRY Look, Fender, look. The seams is all rotten. Look, the lining is like ribbons. Look, the material is threadbare.

FENDER A tailor like you, Morry, to make such a fuss. You should be ashamed.

MORRY (*sitting on chair*) The padding is like an old horse blanket.

FENDER Who asks for new padding? Only make the coat good. Who cares about the padding, so long as the coat is warm?

MORRY It can't be done.

FENDER Don't make jokes, Morry.

MORRY If I say it can't be done, it can't be done.

FENDER So, all right, charge a little more.

MORRY Charge! What does charge matter? It can't be done.

FENDER Why are you so hard for, Morry? After all, you can patch with off cuts.

(MORRY *holds head in hands.*)

I am not asking, after all, for West End style; I should look so smart. I don't care how smart. Only mend the coat, Morry.

MORRY Fender, listen to me, Fender. A good coat like I make has got twenty year's wear. I double stitch the seams with best thread, no rubbish. Every stitch I test, (*Bites imaginary thread.*) so it's good and strong. I use good material: crombie, tweed, what you like. The best. I use a lovely lining; someone else would make a wedding dress from it, such a lining I use.

FENDER You use marvellous lining, Morry.

MORRY I make the whole coat, the button-holes, the pockets, everything.

FENDER Don't I tell everybody? Morry – a needle like Paganini. I tell everybody.

MORRY I would make you such a coat for cost, Fender.

FENDER How much costs such a coat?

MORRY Three yards, say.

FENDER Say two and a half.

MORRY And lining.

FENDER Don't worry yourself with lining.

MORRY I can make you a good coat for twelve pound.

FENDER You can't mend the old coat?

MORRY Please, Fender, do me a favour.

FENDER I can ask? Twelve pound is money.

MORRY (rises) Listen, Fender. I break my neck: ten pound for the coat. You got ten pound?

FENDER I look like a banker? I can save ten pound.

MORRY So.

FENDER (as he starts to put on his old coat) So. So I'm going to have made a bespoke overcoat.

MORRY Bespoke is good.

FENDER Certainly bespoke. You think I would wear Ranting's rubbish? (Sits on chair.)

MORRY (moving D.S.L. and reaching off-stage for patterns) What material you like?

FENDER I can choose materials?

MORRY (to FENDER with patterns) Here, patterns.

FENDER The grey is not nice for me. The blue is better?

MORRY (fingering the blue material) Blue is nice. You can wear blue for any occasion.

FENDER Nigger brown is smart.

MORRY For a young man.

FENDER Black is always good.

MORRY Black is good, but a nice, dark blue is nicer.

FENDER (rising, and moving D.S. of mattress) Believe me, Morry, I think you are right. The blue is good – and thick. What a material!

MORRY (down to FENDER) I should say. So you can save ten pounds?

FENDER Save? Sure I can save. An old man like me, if I got an overcoat, what do I need? (Moving D.S.C. to 'B'.) If I got a bespoke overcoat, what more can I need? (Exit into darkness D.R.)

3. FENDER *(at 'B', D.S.C.)* I told him, polite, but strong. Mr Ranting, I been with this firm with your father and your uncle so many years. All this time I done the same job; nobody complains. Suddenly business is so bad you have to turn me off? Let him answer that. No good. Excuses, anybody can find excuses. What I ask you, Mr Ranting, is, is it right? Let him answer me that. That's what I should have said. I should have told him off, big as he is. The governor, *(turns U.S. and spits)* I used to give him a handkerchief he should wipe his nose. A little boy crying round the warehouse with his stockings down gives me the sack. Why didn't I tell him? Fender, he says, you got something put by, an insurance policy, something? I got something put by, don't worry. You got no family? Don't worry, I got plenty of family, I got friends. He worries about me. I even got a niece with a boarding-house in Clacton, and can she cook? Lovely weather the whole time. *(Turns U.S.C. and then back to audience.)* Mind you, Morry is a good friend. In the morning I put on my new coat. I go to Ranting. I tell him. Give me that coat with the sheepskin. *(Coughs.)* Funny thing, a cough like this, comes right through you. Like a bowl of soup. It flies up through you like a flying jacket. There he goes. *(He traces the path of the imaginary jacket round the theatre. It returns as the threatening celluloid collars.* FENDER *is dying.)* Seventeen dozen cellaloid collars, cellaloid makes with a C, not S – or S, no C. *(Weakly.)* Funny thing, I don't seem to know nothing any more. *(Sinks down as the lights slowly fade.)*

Understanding the play

Characters

Although these three scenes have been isolated from the whole play, you will find, when you read them through, that they form a coherent whole. The dialogue is well written and you will probably find it easy to speak.

Only two characters are involved, but that does not mean that only two people in your group will be needed to bring the play to life. This is an ideal play for giving everyone a chance to act or to produce. You might choose a different Morry for each scene and a different Fender. In fact you might divide your whole group up into those who want to play Fender and those who see themselves in the part of Morry, and give everyone a chance to perform.

Having read the scenes through, either aloud or silently, it would be a good idea to discuss the two characters in detail. They are both three-dimensional people – in other words, both are shown as rounded characters with different sides to their natures, not as pasteboard figures with only one aspect revealed – and both present some problems for the actor.

The men are Jewish. In some groups there will be Jewish boys or girls who will know how Morry and Fender would speak, even if they themselves do not speak with an accent. (The play is set in the East End of London.) They will be able to advise on the way the parts should be spoken. If you have no one in your group who has a good ear for an accent, be sure that you don't fall into the trap of making Fender and Morry sound like Jewish variety comedians. That would ruin the play. Better too little rather than too much accent is the golden rule when acting.

MORRY: is a tailor, a craftsman who loves his work for its own sake; he doesn't do it just for the money. Therefore, in the first scene, anyone playing the part must show the man's pride in his skill. 'I can run you up a pair of trousers from lining canvas you can walk up Saville Road nobody can tell you from the Prince of Wales,' he says. Then, in the next scene, we see him handling his patterns of material with expert hands. This side of his character must be brought out. Morry's love for Fender and his grief at his death also have to be conveyed, and his twinge of conscience because he was not able to finish the bespoke overcoat in time.

FENDER: is a clerk in a clothing warehouse. He deals with anything from sheepskin jackets to celluloid collars. He is old, ill, poor, and yet he faces life with humour and courage. He feels that he shares this attitude with his friend and that gives him the courage to want to go on living. The part must not be acted in a self-pitying way; the least suggestion of a whine would be fatal. Once a character shows that he is sorry for himself, the onlookers lose all sympathy for him. Fender has a death scene to play; he has to suggest that his mind is wandering at the end. Those choosing to play Fender must keep their acting simple and sincere; don't overdo it and drag out the scene. It will be most moving if acted with true feeling.

Both parts need to be spoken with understanding of what is behind the lines. Here are some questions that you could ask yourselves in discussion:

1 *What lines show Morry's love of his craft?*
2 *Where does Morry show that his conscience is troubling him?*
3 *How does the playwright show Fender's courage?*
4 *Where, exactly, in Fender's dying speech does he become delirious?*

How the playwright mixes his ingredients

A good playwright is like a good cook – he knows how to blend different ingredients skilfully. Wolf Mankowitz has described his play as 'a sustained, typically overlong Jewish joke – than which there is no sadder and no funnier story'.

Look through the scenes before you start acting them and see if you can find:

(a) Lines which make you smile. Try to discover how the author mixes in the ingredient of humour.

(b) How the author gets his humorous effect in Morry's first speech through repetition of a phrase; through exaggeration.

(c) Lines which make you sad. Try to discover how the author uses the ingredient of sadness.

(d) How the author uses the ingredient of pathos in the scene where Fender is dying.

You will find, when you speak the lines, that humour can arise from the rhythm and repetition of the dialogue: for example, 'you're a good tailor'; also from incongruity: for example, the ludicrous picture that is conjured up of Fender walking up 'Saville Road' in a pair of trousers made from lining canvas and being mistaken for the Prince of Wales. See if you can find two examples of the same kind of exaggeration in the following scene (2).

Notice especially the directions in italics. When people read plays they often ignore these. This is a mistake, as often the manner in which the scene should be played is described in them. The way to speak two or three pages of dialogue is sometimes suggested in one short stage direction and if you ignore it, you may misinterpret the playwright's intention.

In order to read a play properly you should be able to see the stage in your imagination all the time you are reading and to people it with the characters behaving as the playwright intends. Your stage directions are often your most valuable clue to his intentions.

In the last scene you will find a helpful stage direction towards the end of the speech which indicates exactly when Fender becomes delirious and this will give you the key to the way to speak the lines that follow. Notice how Fender's courage is suggested earlier in this speech: 'Don't worry, I got plenty of family, I got friends . . . I even got a niece with a boarding-house in Clacton, and can she cook? Lovely weather the whole time.' The pathos arises from the contrast between Fender's courage here and his desperate state at the end of the speech.

When you are producing a play, you should try to understand the different ingredients that the playwright has used in making it. When you are acting in a play you should try to bring out these different qualities in your performance.

Bringing the play to life

Once you have discussed the characters and thought about the
playwright's skill in mixing ingredients, you can start to bring
these scenes to life by acting them. I have already mentioned the
kind of accent that you will have to use, but don't forget the
movement of the characters, which will be conditioned by their
age and by their occupations. Fender, the warehouse clerk, might
have a stoop from bending over his books; Morry, the tailor, will
handle his materials and patterns with a professional touch. You
have probably seen tailors at work, either in real life or in films or
on television. If not, you will have to find out their methods and
characteristics in order to be convincing as Morry.

I have suggested that you could divide your entire group into
Morrys and Fenders. Everyone could pair off as far as possible and
work in couples with perhaps a producer to help. Each pair could
work independently and then it would be interesting for all the
scenes to be acted in the classroom. The great advantage of this
play for the classroom is that no scenery is needed and very little
room, so that it could be played in a space cleared in front of the
desks. As each pair acts out their scene or scenes, the rest could
watch and give constructive criticism afterwards.

If you wanted to go on to produce the play for a more public
performance, (for the rest of the school, for example) you could
choose the most convincing Morry and the most convincing Fender
(they need not necessarily have been in the same pair) and decide
which producer had done the best job on the scenes and let him
produce them either in the whole play or in the three scenes already
rehearsed. If you choose to play the three scenes given here, it
would be a good idea to have a linking narrator who could introduce
the first scene, link the other two with some narrative written by
someone in the group and, finally, round the performance off.

Criticism

However you decide to bring the play to life, you should discuss
the final performance in a *post mortem* session aimed at answering
such questions as:

1 Did we believe that Morry was a tailor?
2 Did we believe that Fender was a warehouse clerk?
3 How convincing was the accent? Was it sustained throughout or was it more pronounced in some places than in others?
4 Was the humour brought out in the right way? Or was it overdone, so that the effects were too obvious or insincere?
5 Did the sad and pathetic moments ring true?
6 Did Fender appear cold, ill and tired?

Follow-up

Having worked on these scenes, you may want to go on to perform the whole play for a larger audience. It would be a good choice for a small drama group, as it needs only a cast of four (the other two are Ranting, the owner of the warehouse, and a clerk), and very little in the way of scenery and props. The lighting should be directed on to the character or characters who are speaking, leaving the rest of the acting area in comparative darkness.

If you have been interested in these characters and in the way the dialogue has been written, it might be rewarding to think of two other characters in different circumstances and to write dialogue and scenes for them.

For example, you might write scenes for:

1 Two Welshmen (they could be miners).
2 Two West Country farmers.
3 Two 'Geordies'.
4 Two business men from any part of the country (but it would be best to choose a town that you know. Why?)

Try to link the situation to the men's work and interests. Alternatively, you could write scenes for two women characters:

5 A hospital sister and a nurse.
6 A fashion buyer and a saleswoman.
7 An air hostess and a receptionist at an airport.
8 A woman magazine editor and one of her staff.

The way these characters speak will differ according to where

you place them, but you should make your plot hinge on something to do with their work and, if possible, try to blend in the two
ingredients of humour and sadness that you have seen demonstrated
in *The Bespoke Overcoat*. Having done this, you could take one of
the situations and introduce different ingredients – suspense and
mystery, or worry, leading to relief and happiness.

Christopher Columbus

Louis MacNeice

This radio play was commissioned to celebrate the four hundred and fiftieth anniversary of the discovery of America. The scenes given here are taken from the second (and last) act and show Columbus's triumphant return to Europe in 1493 and his arrival at the Court of Barcelona, where he tells Queen Isabella and King Ferdinand that he has brought them a new world.

Nine years earlier, at the beginning of the play, Columbus is trying to get support for his voyage of discovery; no one will listen to him or take him seriously, and he has to beg even for food and drink. Eventually, he manages to get an audience with Queen Isabella of Spain and asks her to give him a ship. She refers his case to a Royal Commission but, after three days of deliberation, it refuses to give Columbus its official approval. All his hopes are defeated; he is in despair.

We next see him several years later. He has returned to Cordoba to see Beatriz, whom he loves, to tell her that he is leaving Spain, disillusioned with Isabella and her vain promises of help. But before he goes, he sees the old Prior who had helped him before and who now urges him to speak to the Queen again as she enters Granada which has been newly captured from the Moors. This time he is successful and Isabella agrees to appoint a second Royal Commission. When he is turned down for the second time, he goes over its head to the Queen, who promises to give him three ships and to finance his voyage.

In Act II Columbus embarks on his voyage, and is besieged with doubts and fears as day follows day and no land is seen. His crew threaten mutiny unless he turns back, but, at the eleventh hour, land is seen in the distance. Columbus and his crew are welcomed to the shores of the western world by a crowd of Indians.

Our scenes take up the story back in Europe at the point when the Prior, Beatriz, and the Queen hear the news that Columbus has returned having found land in the west.

The play is an account of one man's faith in his vision and his courage in following it through in spite of mockery, indifference and hostility. During the voyage a chorus of doubt and a chorus of faith reflect the man's inward struggle with himself. The chorus may be used in different ways by the playwright. In *Henry V*, Shakespeare used a Chorus, though reduced to one character, to introduce the play and to link the acts. In Greek drama, the chorus were very often used as commentators on what was happening in the play, and emphasised their speeches with the aid of movement. In *Christopher Columbus*, Louis MacNeice uses the choruses in a special way, to tell the listeners what is going on in Columbus's mind. The chorus takes us, in imagination, inside Columbus's brain and enables us to hear the arguments between the two conflicting sides of his nature.

Radio lends itself very well to this intimate kind of speaking. The microphone is sensitive and can easily pick up whispered words and small sounds.

You will notice at once that this play is written in a completely different style from the five other plays in this book. Louis Mac-Neice was a poet and he used an irregular blank verse for the dialogue in *Christopher Columbus*. It is based on the rhythms of ordinary speech, but heightened or flattened according to what is required. Don't let this put you off speaking the lines naturally and on no account use 'poetry voices' – I mean by this a self-conscious stilted, 'voice-beautiful' way of speaking. However, you should study the way that the poet has divided his words into lines and try to mark where each line ends when you speak it, rather than running the lines into each other as in prose.

At a first reading aloud, the chorus lines will probably be ragged, but with practice you will find that a group can manage to speak lines clearly and keep well together.

From the play

(The scene is the shore of Europe.)

HIDALGO What are you doing there, fellow?

PEASANT Eh?

HIDALGO What are you doing perched up there on that rock
Straining your eyes on the sea?
I've been watching you, my man;
You've been stuck up there an hour.

PEASANT I've been stuck up here for weeks.

HIDALGO What for, my man, what for?

PEASANT I'm keeping a look-out.

HIDALGO A look-out?

PEASANT Aye, I come from Cordoba.

HIDALGO Cordoba? What's that got to do with it?

PEASANT 'Twas a lady in Cordoba sent me here.
She told me for to keep look-out.

HIDALGO Stop talking like an idiot.
What did this lady in Cordoba send you here to
look out for?

PEASANT Why, for Señor Columbus.

HIDALGO Señor . . . ? Nombre de Dios!
You mean Columbus that sailed to the West last
year?

PEASANT Aye, that be the one.

HIDALGO And you mean to say you're sitting here
Day after day, week after week,
Waiting for *him*! You're mad,
As mad as Columbus himself.

PEASANT Doña Beatriz – she had a dream.

HIDALGO A dream! She must have had several.
Your Señor Columbus will never come back to
Spain.
We all knew that when he sailed.

PEASANT No matter. I keep my look-out.
The lady in Cordoba pays me.

HIDALGO I hope she pays you well.
Columbus, you see, will never come back to
Europe.

Columbus will never come back – not in a
thousand years.
(*Music answers back Hidalgo and prepares you for
the Return.*)

VASCO Heard the news?
LUÍS What news, Vasco?
VASCO Columbus be back.
LUÍS *Who* be back?
VASCO Columbus. Christopher Columbus. He just put
into port.

PRIOR Heard the news, Brother Antonio?
ANTONIO What news, Father Prior?
PRIOR Our friend Columbus is back. He has found his
land in the West.
ANTONIO I always knew he would. Thank God!
PRIOR Thank God!

CLERIC Have you heard the news, Your Grace?
TALAVERA What news, Señor?
CLERIC Christopher Columbus has arrived in Palos.
TALAVERA I do not believe it, Señor.
CLERIC And what is more, he has found his land in the
West.
TALAVERA I tell you, I do not believe it.

WAITING WOMAN Doña Beatriz! Doña Beatriz!
BEATRIZ Yes, what is it?
WAITING WOMAN Have you heard the news?
BEATRIZ Yes, Maria, I have.
(*Pause.*)
I heard it before anyone.
WAITING WOMAN And what are you going to do?
BEATRIZ Do, Maria? Nothing.
(*Pause.*)
If he comes through Cordoba perhaps I will watch
from the window.

ISABELLA Heard the news, Marquesa?
MARQUESA What news, Your Majesty?
ISABELLA Columbus has come back.

G

MARQUESA Columbus has come back!

ISABELLA Yes, my friend, and he's found it.

MARQUESA Found . . . *it?*

ISABELLA Found what we hoped he would. God is great.

MARQUESA And where is Columbus now?

ISABELLA In Seville. Waiting instructions.

MARQUESA Then he will come to the Court?
He will come here to Barcelona?

ISABELLA Yes, he will come to Barcelona.

(Processional music anticipates the procession.)

ONLOOKER Here they come now, here they come now,
The long procession leaving the gates of Seville,
En route for Barcelona.
Have a good look, ladies and gentlemen, never again
Will this city of Seville see such a wild to-do.
Look at the shining soldiers bearing coffers of gold,
Look at the tattered banners bleached with the brine,
Look at the red savages crowned with feathers –
Gold rings in their noses and popinjays on their shoulders –
Look at the golden masks, the pearls and mother-of-pearl,
And look at who comes here—the Discoverer himself,
The man who is now the talk of Europe, the Very Magnificent Lord
Admiral of the Ocean Sea, Viceroy of the Western World,
With his pale face and his burning eyes, sitting his horse
Like a Roman Emperor . . . or
It might be fitter to say like the fifth
Horseman of the Apocalypse.

(The procession draws level. Columbus's followers are chanting in the manner of a Round.)

Back from the West

Beyond the world
Back from the West

We have returned
Beyond the world
Back from the West

And here we are
We have returned
Beyond the world
Back from the West

And here we are
We have returned
Beyond the world

And here we are
We have returned

And here we are!

ALL TOGETHER Back from the West
Beyond the world
We have returned
And here we are.

SPOKESMAN
OF PROCESSION From Seville over the Sierras, bound for the Royal
Court,
By a dusty road to the banks of the Guadalquivir,
To a Moorish city of winding streets and gardens
Set among groves of olive and orange,
Here we come in our Admiral's train
Bearing the wealth of the West and the news of
the Indies
Here we come to Cordoba, here
Through Cordoba we come riding.
(*As the cheers of the onlookers recede you notice
Doña Beatriz in a balcony.*)
WAITING WOMAN Doña Beatriz! Doña Beatriz! Did you see him?
BEATRIZ Yes, but he didn't see *me*.
He rode by in the way that he would –

Looking neither to right nor to left.

WAITING WOMAN This is a day for him!

A day of triumph.

BEATRIZ A day – I would say – of miracle.

But he will die unhappy.

(*The music surges back, Beatriz is left behind and we ride on with Columbus.*)

SPOKESMAN
OF PROCESSION From Cordoba we go on, from Cordoba to Montoro,

From Montoro to Jaén huddled on wooded hills,

From Jaén to Orihuela on the banks of the Segura

And thence to Alicante with its palm-trees by the sea;

And everywhere the crowds come out to meet us and they throw

Flowers upon our heads and we ride on

With our Indians and our popinjays and gold;

We ride on, ride on.

CHORUS Back from the West

Beyond the world

We have returned

And here we are.

SPOKESMAN
OF PROCESSION And now we come to the great white port of Valencia

With its multitude of roofs and its towering campanile

And the people of Valencia bring us flowers and bring us fruit,

Blow us kisses as we were lovers and look up to us as gods –

And we smile the smile of gods and we ride on.

And we come to Catalunya, to Roman Tarragona,

With its dark cobbled alleys clambering up the hill

And the smell of fish and wine

And the broken Roman arches that betoken

So much glory of the past

Which is nothing to the glory that is ours

That surrounds us as we ride to the King and Queen of Spain

Holding court in Barcelona . . .

HERALD Holding court in Barcelona!
(The processional music ends and silence intro-
duces the Court at Barcelona.)

ISABELLA Señor Don Christopher Columbus!
We Isabella, Queen of Castile and Aragon,
Do here before the assembled peers of our land
Welcome you back to Spain and give you our royal
thanks
For that against the odds you have done what you
have done
To the greater glory of God and the honour of
Spain.
Of your achievements we have already heard
And here we see their tangible evidence –
The gold, the pearls, and these strange men;
But we ask you now, Señor, out of your own
mouth
Here to address the Crown and the Peers of Spain –
Aye, and the whole of the serried Christian world –
And tell us your own story and what it means.

COLUMBUS Your Catholic Majesties . . . it is hard for me
On such a day and before such an audience,
Feeling myself on a pinnacle high among clouds of
dream,
To find the words – it is hard to find the words
For a theme that no man yet has phrased or
painted –
The passage where no passage lay,
The world where no world was before.
But this is what I have done:
I took three ships and sailed them into the teeth
of the West,
Into what seemed the certainty of death
And against the veto of Nature.
Weeks went by and no land came, I might have
Well turned back but I did not, I went on
And in the ripeness of God's will I found
The second Earthly Paradise and there
I raised the cross of Christ and the banner of
Castile.
Your Majesties, look out yonder,
Look out yonder along the line of my arm

Across Tibidabo and the hills of Spain:
Four thousand miles out there to the West
Lie uncharted lands – they are yours to chart,
Uncounted treasure – yours for the taking,
Aye and countless hordes of heathen men
Who are from now your subjects,
Unenlightened souls who wait the light.
Aye, your Majesties, this new world
That I have opened up through the will of God –
Only God can tell what is its total worth,
And God alone knows what it will become
Or what may be the blessings that late or soon
May flow from thence to Europe –
Aye, and to all mankind from this new world.
This is my story and this is what it means:
Here and now at your court in Barcelona
In the year of Our Lord Fourteen-Hundred-And-
Ninety-Three,
Before the Throne of Spain and the eyes and ears
of Europe
And before the crowded jury of posterity –
I have brought you a new world.
(*The crowd then sing in triumph.*)

LEADER   Glory, glory to God.
Joy in the land of Spain.
They sailed away to the West,
Now they are here again.

CHORUS   Glory, glory to God.
Joy in the land of Spain.

LEADER   They sailed away to the West,
Now they are here again.
They tracked the sun to his lair,
They found the Golden Main.

CHORUS   They sailed away to the West,
Now they are here again.
COLUMBUS   (*calling from distance*)
I have brought you a new world.

LEADER   That world that we have found
Shall never be lost again.
The voyage that we made –
We made it not in vain.

CHORUS   The world that we have found
Shall never be lost again.

Understanding the play

Characters

HIDALGO: a Spanish gentleman.

PEASANT
VASCO } all need to be broader in speech than Hidalgo.
LUÍS

THE PRIOR: is a kindly old man, the head of a monastery. He should speak with authority.

TALAVERA: is the Queen's confessor. All through, he has had no faith in Columbus and thought that his ideas were sacrilegious. Even now, he does not believe that Columbus has really found land in the west.

BEATRIZ: lives in Cordoba. Although she loves Columbus, she realizes:

> Though he is my love
> He is not for me;
> What he loves is over
> Loveless miles of sea
> Haunted by the West,
> Eating out his heart –
> When will he return?
> Only to depart.

It was she who told the peasant to keep a look-out on a rock by the sea shore for Columbus's ships.

ISABELLA: is Queen of Spain and married to King Ferdinand. She is a Catholic, a woman of tremendous dignity and power, which must be suggested in the bearing and speech of whoever plays her. The Spanish Court at that time was one of the most glittering in Europe. The Spaniards of those days loved pomp and ceremony. The Court was thronged with richly dressed courtiers and envoys from other countries were frequent visitors. Try to find pictures illustrating the costume of the time.

MARQUESA: is a close friend of Isabella, in fact, the only woman whom she trusts. She is sympathetic to Columbus's cause, a warm-hearted and impetuous woman.

ONLOOKER: has a very important part to play. He or she has to describe the procession of soldiers carrying coffers of gold, the Red Indians in all their finery and Columbus himself and his followers as they march from the gates of Seville en route for Barcelona. The Onlooker has to see everything vividly in his imagination in order that we, too, can see what he describes. His lines need to be spoken with punch and at a brisk tempo in much the same way as if he were giving a modern running commentary on some sporting event or on a procession like the Lord Mayor's Show.

SPOKESMAN OF THE PROCESSION: has two important speeches. He has to show, in his voice, the exultation that every one of Columbus's followers feels. In his second speech, he has to conjure up for us the white port of Valencia with its welcoming crowds and the dark cobbled alleys of Tarragona full of the smell of fish and wine. The speech has to build up to the climax of the final lines describing:

> . . . the glory that is ours
> That surrounds us as we ride to the King and
> Queen of Spain
> Holding court in Barcelona . . .

COLUMBUS: has only one speech in these scenes, but this is one of great importance; in fact, it is the climax of the play. Columbus is a man with an almost mystical faith in his mission. We see him here at the moment of triumph, to which he has been striving through years of failure and despair. You will notice that the lines themselves build up gradually to the climax of the last sentence:

> I have brought you a new world.

Columbus is a difficult part to play, but if the lines are spoken with feeling and yet control, so that the shape of the speech leading gradually up to the climax is kept, the speaker should enjoy playing it.

The radio playwright's task

What are the special problems of the radio playwright as compared with those of the writer for the theatre?

Before acting the scenes, you will find it worthwhile to discuss the following points:

1 *The effect on radio must be got by sound and sound alone. The radio writer has to think, all the time, of how the words will sound in the mouths of the actors.*

2 *The radio writer has to be more economical than the theatre playwright, because he generally has much less time at his disposal (usually from half an hour to an hour).*

3 *As the speakers are not seen, their identity has to be established far more strongly than in the theatre, where the audience can see the actors.*

4 *As the radio writer gets no help from scenery, he has to convey strongly to the listener the places where things are happening – by the use of words, and of music and sound effects generally.*

All these things seem to make the radio writer's work more difficult than that of the theatre playwright. But he has certain advantages:

(*a*) He can journey from place to place and from century to century more easily than in the theatre. There is no need for blackouts, changes of scenery, etc.

(*b*) He can handle a large chorus of voices much more easily than on a stage.

(*c*) He can get the effect of up-to-the-minute happenings through the use of running commentaries.

Read through the scenes again and see if you can find out how Louis MacNeice solved his problems of:

(*a*) Creating atmosphere through the words that the actor speaks. Notice, particularly, the Spokesman of the Procession's two speeches.

(*b*) The need for economy. Notice how atmosphere is built up by a series of very short scenes between two people.

(*c*) Making the identity of various characters known at once. For example:

PRIOR Heard the news, Brother Antonio?
ANTONIO What news, Father Prior?

(*d*) Suggesting situations by means of music and sound effects and the words of the actors. Notice, for example, the treatment of the procession and the opening lines of Hidalgo.

Now see if you can find how the writer made use of his advantages over the theatre playwright. Pick out examples of:

1 *Swift transference from place to place.*
2 *Use of a chorus.*
3 *The use of a running commentary technique.*

Bringing the play to life

There are two ways of doing this with the scenes from *Christopher Columbus*:

(*a*) you can rehearse it as a radio play and tape-record the scenes when you are satisfied that you have achieved a reasonable result;

(*b*) you can rehearse it for a stage presentation with movement and grouping.

Some of the scenes chosen in this book need very little acting space, and could easily be done in the classroom. But, obviously, *Columbus* needs to be rehearsed in a hall to get the full effect of the processions and the dignity of the scene at the Court of Barcelona, where large numbers are involved. You may decide to work on the play as for a radio performance to begin with, and then go on to perform the scenes with movement, for an audience who can see you. I have seen the play performed by a school in an arena setting using the central gangway for the processions, and it worked very well. However, whether you work on the scenes as radio drama or as a visual play, the emphasis in each case must be on the words first of all.

Criticism

When you listen to your version of the play on a tape-recorder, make a special note of the following points for discussion afterwards:

1 Was sufficient difference made between the Spanish gentleman's voice and the peasant's in the first sequence?
2 Did the Prior really sound like an old man?
3 Did the Marquesa's enthusiasm come over in her few lines?
4 Did the Onlooker capture the true running commentary style in the description of the procession leaving the gates of Seville?
5 Was the Chorus well together and distinct?
6 Did the Spokesman of the Procession capture the triumphant feeling of Columbus's followers in his two speeches?
7 Was Isabella convincing as the Queen of Spain?
8 Did Columbus manage to shape and control his speech without losing the feeling that is in the lines?

Follow-up

You may decide to read the whole play and even to perform it all eventually. Perhaps you will want to find out more about the playwright. Most modern anthologies of poetry contain examples of MacNeice's work. You will find that he uses an almost conversational style and that many of his poems are easy to speak aloud.

Having worked on a radio play, you may feel inspired to try to write one of your own. It could be an individual or a class effort, but always bear in mind the restrictions – and the advantages – of your medium. Above all, remember that radio drama's raw material is words in the mouths of speakers. You should imagine that you are communicating with a wide audience, so make your treatment broadly dramatic and very clear. Finally, use your sound effects discreetly, and don't forget the danger of overdoing them. Let those 'BBC seagulls' be a warning to you!

Here are some suggestions for short tape plays that you might write yourselves:

1 An account of the Everest expedition, treated in the same way as Christopher Columbus and perhaps using the same device of choruses to convey the climbers' thoughts.
2 A story set on a rocket station, where there has been a series of disappointments, but which ends in success.
3 An episode from English history: for example, an account of a battle told as it is happening by some of the soldiers and commanders.

Conclusion

In these six plays you have seen people tackling different problems, some of which may have had particular application to you yourself.

You have seen some of the different ways in which dramatists work.

Whether your enthusiasm is for writing, production, acting or criticism, I hope that you will have been encouraged to take an interest in what is being written for the theatre today; for the theatre always mirrors 'the very age and body of the time, his form and pressure'.

Published plays by the authors of the extracts in this book:

John Osborne

Look Back in Anger
Luther
Plays for England
The Entertainer
Epitaph for George Dillon (with Anthony Creighton)
Inadmissible Evidence
(Published by Evans Brothers Limited)

The World of Paul Slickey
A Bond Honoured
A Subject of Scandal and Concern (television play)
(Published by Faber & Faber)

Arnold Wesker

Chicken Soup with Barley
I'm Talking about Jerusalem
Roots
(Published by Evans Brothers Limited)

Chips with Everything
The Kitchen
The Four Seasons
Their Very Own and Golden City
(Published by Jonathan Cape Limited)

Wolf Mankowitz

Five One Act Plays
Expresso Bongo
(Published by Evans Brothers Limited)

Willis Hall

The Long and the Short and the Tall
A Glimpse of the Sea
(Published by Evans Brothers Limited)

Keith Waterhouse & Willis Hall

Billy Liar
Celebration
All Things Bright and Beautiful
England Our England
The Sponge Room & Squat Betty
Come Laughing Home
(Published by Evans Brothers Limited)

Louis MacNeice

Christopher Columbus
Out of the Picture
The Mad Island (radio play)
The Administrator (radio play)
(Published by Faber & Faber)